BUD & LOU

BUD & LOU

The Abbott & Costello Story

by

BOB THOMAS

J. B. Lippincott Company
Philadelphia & New York

U.S. Library of Congress Cataloging in Publication Data

Thomas, Bob, birth date
  Bud & Lou : the Abbott & Costello story.

  Filmography: p.
  1. Abbott, Bud, 1895–1974. 2. Costello, Lou.
3. Comedians—United States—Biography. I. Title.
PN2287.A217T5   791.43′028′0922 [B]   76–54743
ISBN–0–397–01195–4

Contents

List of Illustrations

Acknowledgments

THE AUTHOR is grateful to many persons for their kindness in sharing their memories and viewpoints of the lives of Bud Abbott and Lou Costello. Among them: Betty (Mrs. Bud) Abbott, Norman Abbott, Olive Abbott, Glen Adams, Steve Allen, Robert Arthur, Charles Barton, Milton Berle, Joe Besser, William Bowers, Milton Bronson, Red Buttons, Candy Candido, Kenneth Carter, Howard Christie, Robert Cohn, Pat Costello, Morris Davis, Ralph Edwards, Bobby Faye, Alex Gottlieb, Betty Abbott Griffin, Ralph Handley, Edmund Hartman, Bob Hope, Danny Kaye, Jesse Kaye, Joe Kenny, Earl Kenton, Marie Costello Kirk, Howard Koch, Sid Kuller, Charles Lamont, Boo LaVon, Helen Howard Lewis, Arthur Lubin, Eddie Lynch, Sidney Miller, Harold Minsky, Lew Rachmil, Martin Ragaway, Kate Smith, Leonard Spigelgass, Leonard Stern, Sam Weisbord.

Most of all, I thank Eddie Sherman, faithful manager of Bud and Lou over the years, and witness to many of the events chronicled in this book. His insights and recollections provided the necessary key to understanding the A&C story.

In fairness to those mentioned above, I must add that they should not be held responsible for the interpretations and conclusions included herein. That responsibility rests solely with the author.

Bud Abbott was a genius. Lou Costello was one of the greatest comics in movies; his "scare take" was the best I've ever seen. Together Bud and Lou were sublimely funny.

—MEL BROOKS

BUD & LOU

1

Abbott and Costello Meet Franklin Delano Roosevelt

THE HOTEL BALLROOM was boisterously male. Gray-purple panatela haze lingered a few feet above the white-linen tablecloths. Warm, sweaty smells exuded from the starched shirts and satin-trimmed tuxedos. Military uniforms added to the maleness of the occasion. Important uniforms, bearing four and five stars. It was a democratic gathering, Supreme Court justices and reporters, war industry magnates and corporals, senators, cabinet members, news photographers.

A voice on the loudspeaker called over the din: "Gentlemen, the President of the United States!"

Immediately the talking ceased and chairs slid noisily on the ballroom floor as the guests rose and gazed to the dais. The curtain rustled, the two men stepped between the folds. The President was pale but grinning broadly, taking slow, painful paces as he clutched the arm of his son James, tall and tan-faced in a Marine officer's uniform. The hotel orchestra played "Hail to the Chief" as the President hobbled to his chair. He unlocked his braces and sat down, still beaming at the crowd and waving heartily. He motioned for the guests to be seated. Again the chairs scraped on hardwood as the orchestra began playing "You'd Be So Nice to Come Home To." The song fit the evening's mood. At last the war was going well for the Allies, and talk had been turning to when the boys would be coming home.

Midway through the dinner, Mr. Roosevelt turned to the chairman and asked, "Are those fellows Abbott and Costello here tonight?"

"Indeed they are, Mr. President," the newsman replied.

"Well, I'd like to meet those boys."

They were summoned from their table. Both were handsome in their finely tailored tuxedos. Lou seemed uncommonly shy as he approached the dais, Bud had his customary assurance. Mr. Roosevelt half-rose and shook their hands vigorously.

"I've been wanting to meet you chaps," the President began.

Lou seemed unable to reply. "It's an honor for us, Mr. President," said Bud.

"You know," Mr. Roosevelt continued, "I never saw your act in burlesque. My mother wouldn't let me go." He guffawed at the remark, and Bud and Lou joined in the laughter.

"You coulda brought her to our shows," Lou interjected. "Bud and I never talked dirty."

"Well, I'm sorry I missed you on the stage," Mr. Roosevelt said. "But I've seen your comedies in our little theater at the White House, and they're good for what ails me. And I hear you on radio on Thursday nights—that is, when the generals and the admirals aren't keeping me busy."

"That's thrilling to know, Mr. President," said Bud with a wide grin.

"Of course Eleanor wonders why I laugh so much; she doesn't get the jokes." The President guffawed again, then turned serious. "Henry Morgenthau tells me that you two are the best salesmen for war bonds that he's got. I want you to know that your country appreciates all the work you've done."

"Well, we have to serve some way, Mr. President," said Bud. "I'm too old for the army."

"And I'm too fat," Lou added.

Mr. Roosevelt laughed appreciatively. "I heard about your illness, Lou. Rheumatic fever, wasn't it?"

16

"Yes, sir," Lou replied.

"Tricky thing. Almost as tricky as infantile paralysis. You take care of yourself, Lou. The country needs you."

"Take care of *your*self, Mr. President. *You're* the one the country needs."

"Will you do me one favor?" Mr. Roosevelt asked.

"Anything," Bud replied.

"Will you do 'Who's on First?' tonight?"

"You got it!" Lou said.

Later in the evening, Bud and Lou ascended to the stage amid heavy applause. After a few well-received jokes, Lou remarked, "We got a special request from the Prez."

"Lou, I'm ashamed of you," Bud said.

"What'd I do now?" Lou asked.

"Honestly, referring to him as 'the Prez'!"

"That's better than what the Republicans call him." The laughter was loud, especially from Mr. Roosevelt.

"Now stop that!" Bud snapped. "You must show respect when you're invited to a gathering like this. Just look out there and what do you see?"

"A bunch of stuffed shirts," Lou replied. Much laughter.

"Don't talk like that. These newspapermen invited you to their banquet and you act like a guttersnipe. Have you no manners? Have you no sense of decorum? What have you got to say for yourself?"

Lou gazed miserably at the audience, stuck a finger in his mouth, and muttered, "I'm a ba-a-a-ad boy!" Laughter and applause.

"Now what were you trying to say?" Bud asked.

"I was trying to say that the Prez—I'm sorry, Abbott—that the Commander-in-Chief hasn't had time to go to the baseball park because he's too busy winning the war. So he'd like you to tell him who's playing for the Washington Senators these days."

"I'd be glad to. But you'll have to listen carefully. You see, a lot of the regular players are away in the service, and the new ones have some strange names."

17

"Okay, tell me their names."

"Who's on first, What's on second, and I Don't Know is on third."

"That's what I want you to tell the Prez—the names of the Washington players."

"I'm telling you," Bud insisted. "Who's on first, What's on second, I Don't Know is on third."

"You know the players' names?" Lou asked.

"Yes."

"Well, then, who is playin' first?"

"Yes."

"I mean the fella's name on first base."

"Who."

"The fella's name on first base for the Senators."

"Who."

"The guy on first base."

"*Who* is on first base."

Lou, shouting in exasperation, "Well, what are you askin' me for?" . . .

And so it went, the audience's hilarity mounting with Lou's frustration as he probed further into the lineup.

"Wait a minute," Lou cried. "Tell me the pitcher's name."

"Tomorrow," Bud replied calmly.

"You don't want to tell me today?"

"I told you, Costello."

"Then go ahead."

"Tomorrow."

"I can't stand it! Tell me the catcher's name."

"Today."

"Yeah, today. I can't wait all week."

"I'll tell you his name: Today."

The guests were weak with laughter as the punchlines came in steady succession. Finally the enraged Lou managed a semblance of understanding: "Now I throw the ball to first base, whoever it is drops the ball, so the guy runs to second."

"That's right," said Bud.

"Who picks up the ball and throws to What. What throws

18

it to I Don't Know. I Don't Know throws it back to Tomorrow. A triple play!"

"Yeah, it could be."

"A guy gets up and socks a long fly ball to center. Why? I don't know. And I don't care."

"What did you say?"

"I don't care."

"Oh, that's our shortstop."

As they finished the routine, the sound of male laughter resounded through the ballroom like the noise of an ocean wave. The beaming President waved an arm at the performers. Immensely pleased and proud, Bud and Lou waved back.

2

A Peculiarly
American Institution

THEY FLASHED like twin meteors across a summer sky, dazzling the nation with their bright, brash, totally unsophisticated comedy. Like all great funnymen, their appeal was universal—to all ages, men and women alike, city audiences and the sticks. Their timing was as precise as a heart surgeon's. But technique was not the crucial factor; more important was the interplay of their personalities.

As straight man, Bud Abbott evinced the manners and morals of a carnival grifter. He was the swift-talking, brass-hearted rogue, often the victim of his own chicanery. Lou Costello, the comic, portrayed the victimized Everyman, an innocent in a mendacious world. Together they worked with the harmony of a Heifetz-Piatigorsky duet.

Their attitude was contentious; they were forever seeking advantage of each other. Yet the audience with its unfailing intuition peered through the bickering and the counterplots and recognized the affection that existed between them. Of course it was there. No two men could have risen together from twenty-dollar-a-night club dates through the harsh show world without developing a comradely spirit toward each other. As long as that comradeship remained in evidence, they would prosper. If it was destroyed . . .

Bud and Lou sprang from the toughest, most exacting school for entertainers—and the most American. Burlesque was

lusty, bawdy, noisy, uncouth, like Americans. It was vital, energetic, joyous, and eager to please, like Americans. It had laughter
that rocked the belly and dances that stroked the libido. It was
the poor man's commedia dell'arte, the horny man's solace, the
young man's gateway to a world of mirth and carnality. The
good old times of burlesque came during the Depression. The burlesque house was next door to the soup kitchen, and both
filled man's needs. Every Depression city had its burlesque
theater, and smaller towns, too. In New York City you could
see burlesque day and night for a week and not repeat a show.
There were the Columbia Theater and the Gayety, both on
Times Square, and the Oriental, further up Broadway at 49th
Street. The Irving Place on 14th Street played two-a-day, and
the People's Theater in the Bowery had a grind policy, operating
from morning to midnight. The City was on 14th Street, the
Gotham on 125th. Brooklyn had the Werbas, Star and Oxford,
Newark the Empire, Union City the Hudson.

In the beginning was a circuit called the Columbia Wheel,
and a burlesque artist could find forty weeks of steady work
circling the Wheel from one city to the next. The circuit's
showcase was the Columbia Theater at 47th and Broadway,
and under its protective marquee burlesque people gathered on
the Columbia Beach to exchange lies about their triumphs on
the Wheel. Across Broadway in front of the Palace stood the
vaudeville performers, a step higher on the social ladder. But
their numbers were thinning as vaudeville neared its twilight, and
many concealed their pride and crossed Broadway to test the
waters at the Columbia Beach. Comics who had played the same
act for years on the Orpheum Circuit and Gus Sun Time now
had to learn new routines every week. Ballerinas and adagio
dancers studied how to remove their costumes in provocative
ways. Chorus girls from Fanchon and Marco lines, pretty
things who could tap and toe-dance, replaced the lumpy dancers
of burlesque choruses. There was work for all. The burnt-out
comics and varicose chorines could find jobs in Baltimore and
Memphis and Galveston at the "scratch houses," havens for
over-the-hill artists as well as fleas.

If you were a burlesque comic, you worked in a stock

house or a traveling company. In a stock house you stayed with the same cast for twenty weeks or a full year, a new show every week. Mostly you traveled, sometimes in a company that carried a full cast—sixteen chorus girls, three strippers, two comics, two straight men, a talking woman, and a tits singer (who sang while the chorus strutted its charms), moving from city to city with costumes and scenery in a single railroad car. More often you were accompanied by a cast of four or five, and the local house supplied the chorus line, singer, and resident comic.

You arrived in Boston on a Tuesday and checked into the Commonwealth Hotel, which offered special rates to burlesque people. You walked to the theater after the last performance and started planning the show to open Friday. The strippers gave their music sheets to the orchestra, instructing the drummer on special cues, and you worked out the sketches with the house comic and the stage manager. "Let's do Floogle Street and the Lemon Table and the Mustard," you suggested. Or the Baseball Routine, Lamb Chops, and the Hammer. Or the Apple Bit, the African Dodger, and the Restaurant Scene. If the routines had not been done recently at the theater, the stage manager said okay. Sometimes the local comic, out of nastiness, had done your best routine the week before your arrival, and the routine could not be repeated. Okay. You fixed the bastard by stepping on his laughs and fouling up his props.

You did four shows a day and a midnight performance on Saturday. Five on holidays, too, and New Year's Eve might bring a dozen shows. It was hard work, but the burlesque union insisted on a half-day's pay for every show over four, so you could earn a handsome check on New Year's Eve.

You hoped for rain. A heavy downpour would pull the floaters off the street and into the theater. Otherwise you struggled uphill to win a response from the first audience. They were mostly salesmen and winos and bums seeking shelter. The second show improved in numbers, but they were mostly repeaters who had seen your acts, so you had to clown and ad lib to hold them. The evening show had more bodies, some of them well-dressed and a few female. It was a challenge, then, to make the women laugh; the reward was heart-filling, because if you could get three women to laugh, you captured the whole audience. The late show was the best. You and the straight man had been nipping a few, and so had your audience, and all of you were seeking amusement. There were repeaters, especially in the second half of the show, and noisy drunks, but they were sitting targets for your insults. You yourself were in full control, roaming the stage, antic and reckless, feeling for nerve endings that would generate explosions of laughter.

This was the schooling that prepared Bud and Lou for their conquest of the mass audience.

3

Bud Abbott:
The Early Years

ACT OF AGREEMENT made and entered into this day and date, October 16, 1889, between P. T. Barnum and J. A. Bailey, proprietors of a combined circus, menagerie, etc. This is to certify that I, Harry Abbott, of my own free will and accord, do hereby contract and agree for and in consideration of the sum of $50 a week hereinafter do bind, hire and employ myself to and travel with the shows owned by Barnum and Bailey in any capacity required of me, the same ever being for the specific benefit and profit of the said Barnum and Bailey; to devote my entire time and attention to all and any duties assigned me to the best of my skill, knowledge and ability; to comply with all the rules and regulations of the managers of the Establishment; to refrain from *drunkenness, fighting, stealing or any improper conduct* and so conduct myself in an orderly, lawful and gentlemanly manner.

This engagement or contract to be for the entire winter season of 1889 and 1890 in London, England, and the summer season of 1890 if required, or until the company quits traveling or disbands. . . .

Thus the contract between the Barnum & Bailey Show on the one hand and Harry Abbott on the other. Harry was a "twenty-four-hour man," the energetic fellow who preceded the circus by a day and posted bills all over town, arranged for a clown

24

show at the orphanage, gave the police free tickets to assure a problem-free parade down Main Street. Harry had been born in Pennsylvania of British parentage, joined the circus early as a candy butcher, selling taffy and nougats in the audience. His winning personality and potential as a salesman were soon recognized by the circus owners and he was promoted to twenty-four-hour man. Harry fell in love with a bareback rider, Rae Fisher, a lovely, sweet-tempered girl from a Maryland family of German Jews. They were married, and Rae left the circus to maintain the Abbott home in Asbury Park, New Jersey. Harry returned from his circus travels often enough to father four children: Harry, Jr.; Olive Victoria, named for the queen her father had met when the circus played England; William, born October 2, 1895, and soon named Bud; and Florence, who was always called Babe. When the children were small, Harry moved the family to Coney Island, where they lived for eighteen years.

There were happy times when Harry Abbott came home from the long season's travel with the circus. Mama Abbott ladened the table with steaming dishes of sauerbraten and red cabbage, and she and the four children listened raptly to tales of blizzards in Montana, knife fights among the sideshow freaks, escaped tigers and stampeding elephants. Young Bud enjoyed the stories most of all. He suffered through each winter of school, staring out the window and dreaming of the time when his father would come home and Coney Island would prepare for the summer's entertainment. Many days he escaped from Public School 100 to stroll along the boardwalk and see the signs being repainted, the thrill rides regeared for the onslaught of vacationers from the city.

One year Harry Abbott came home early from the circus so he could operate a Coney Island attraction he called Midget City. While on the road he had enlisted midgets in Barnum & Bailey and other circuses to spend their summer at Coney and appear in a village setting that would be scaled to their size. One day Harry left the construction of his Midget City to glance over the other attractions. Some of them were already operating for the early-season visitors, and he paused to observe the cancan dancers on the outdoor stage at the Moulin Rouge show. He was pleased to see that the operator had hired young and energetic dancers instead of the overweight chorines of the previous summer.

A small crowd, almost entirely male, stood three-deep before the stage. Harry thought he recognized the back of one of the heads. He walked closer and became certain.

"William!" The father used his younger son's given name only in anger.

Bud heard the voice and froze in terror.

"William, aren't you supposed to be in school at this hour?" Harry Abbott demanded.

"Yes, Dad," the boy replied.

"Then why aren't you?"

"Because school is boring."

"Well, you get your little ass back to school before I beat it for you."

Bud returned to his classes, but not for long. He came home from school one day when he was fourteen and announced, "I'm not going back." Harry Abbott was on the road with the circus, and his long-distance threats failed to alter the boy's resolve. Nor could his mother's tears. Bud was in search of a different kind of education, one that couldn't be found in history books and grammars.

Now he could spend all of his days amid the glittering attractions of Coney Island. This was the arena he enjoyed, not the dusty world of books. He loved to wander along the midway and listened to the staccato of the show barkers and the chant of the popcorn and cotton-candy sellers. He was known as Harry Abbott's boy, so he was allowed free admission to the shows and he could even roam backstage and hear the quick talk of the entertainers. He earned his first pay as a performer when he and his brother portrayed the Katzenjammer Kids to attract customers to the Crystal Maze, corridors of mirrors with a hidden exit. Bud knew his way through the passageways, and he earned additional money by guiding confused customers to daylight.

26

Bud shilled for carnivals and worked as a candy butcher, then tried sign painting and moving houses. It was dull, flat, uninspiring work. When his father tired of his circus travels and came home to organize a circuit of burlesque shows, Bud pleaded for a job. At sixteen he was appointed assistant treasurer of the Casino Theater in Brooklyn. He spent as much time backstage and in the theater as he did in the box office. The Casino was far from the bigtime, but it attracted such performers as W. C. Fields, Bert Lahr, Clark and McCullough, Jack Pearl and Fanny Brice, and Bud studied their routines over and over.

Bud was savoring the delights of the adult world, and they included spending a cozy night with a warm-hearted chorus girl or drinking after the show with the comics and straight men he so greatly admired. One night he lingered too long in a Brooklyn bar. That evening he had watched two performances by the comic juggler, W. C. Fields, and he recounted the experience to a chance companion.

"I've never seen anyone so funny in my life," said the enthusiastic Bud.

"So you work at the Casino, eh?" asked the man, who wore a knitted cap, pea jacket and flaring trousers and spoke with a Norwegian accent. He was taller and more strongly built than the husky Bud.

"Yes, sir, I'm the treasur' of the theater," Bud replied, although he was the assistant treasurer. "An' if you ever are in port an' wanna see the burlesque show, jus' ask for me, Bud Abbott. I'll see that you get a pass."

"That's very kind of you, young man. I'd like to buy you another drink."

That was all Bud remembered. He awoke groggily, unsurely, not wanting to open his eyes because of the pain in his head. So this is what it's like to have a hangover, he thought. It felt so bad that the bed seemed to be rocking. Then he suddenly realized: it *was* rocking. His eyes blinked open, and he saw that he lay in the bunk of a tiny metal room. He rushed to the porthole and saw nothing but limitless sea.

The door was locked and Bud pounded on it until he heard

footsteps approach. He saw the ruddy face of the man in the bar. "What the hell has happened?" Bud demanded.

"Well, now," the man said with a smile, "I thought a strong lad like you would enjoy an ocean voyage."

"You mean you shanghaied me? Why, you—"

Bud swung his fist but the smiling sailor intercepted it in his large hand. "You'd better save your energy for shoveling coal. You'll be doing a lot of that aboard the *Christinfjord*."

Bud's anger soon subsided, and he accepted the work routine aboard the Norwegian freighter. It was his nature, as we shall see later in his relations with Lou Costello, to accept the inevitable and not to rage over injustices that had been committed against him. He exacted a minor degree of revenge in the English-language classes he conducted for the Norwegian sailors. The way to thank an American or Englishman, he informed his fellow voyagers, was to say, "Fuck you." The sailors repeated the phrase. In his bunk at night Bud smiled as he contemplated what would happen when the Norwegians followed his instructions in New York or London.

Bud worked his way back across the Atlantic and hurried home to Coney Island for a tearful reunion with his family. His mother had cried every day during his absence, not knowing whether her younger son was alive or dead.

He returned to the Casino Theater in Brooklyn, then began the travels that would take him throughout the country for the next twenty years.

Bud landed in Washington, D.C., as treasurer of the National Theater. It was a responsible position for a young man of nineteen, but the word had passed along the burlesque circuit that Harry Abbott's boy was bright, eager, and trustworthy. Indeed, Bud did an expert job of taking care of the box office receipts and the payroll, finishing early so he could spend time backstage. He enjoyed hearing the straight men and comics exchange yarns about life on the road, and he liked talking to the dancers. A new girl at the National caught his eye. She was a pretty thing, seventeen, with a trim, athletic figure. She called herself Betty Smith, though her name at birth in Buffalo had

Salad days in burlesque: Bud (on the right) as the sharpie ... and as the cop

*The young Mr. Abbott—
dapper is the only word*

been Jenny Mae Pratt. Like Bud, she had left home early, and she had traveled with a Japanese acrobatic team and with Smith and Smith, a wire act.

After Bud had known Betty Smith two weeks, both were invited for a cruise on the Potomac aboard the yacht of a rich young man. He had an eye for the beauties of the National chorus, and had become friends with Bud so he could be introduced to them. Bud brought along Betty and two other dancers from the show for the cruise.

It was Sunday, the only day of rest for burlesque people, since the blue laws kept the theaters closed. The September sun shone lazily on the Potomac, and the young men and women reclined on the upper deck, munching sandwiches and sipping mint juleps. This was the way he would like to live some day, Bud reflected.

One of the girls was Billie Jackson, an exuberant personality both on the stage and off. "It's such a beautiful day, I'm going for a swim," she announced. Before anyone could stop her, she had peeled down to her bloomers and dived into the river.

The others watched in amusement as she bobbled in the water. Then Bud noticed that she was retreating swiftly from the boat. A swift current was taking her toward Chesapeake Bay, and it was impossible to swing the boat around to overtake her. Bud pulled off his shoes and jumped into the water.

"Help me! Help me!" Billie cried. Her friends on the deck shouted encouragement as Bud swam toward her in swift, strong strokes. He reached her and put an arm under her chin. When the soaked pair were pulled on board, Billie was hysterical with fright, and the others tried to calm her. Betty Smith had eyes only for the rescuer. She decided immediately that Bud Abbott, the tall, debonair, heroic nineteen-year-old, had all the qualities she admired in a man.

A week later, on September 17, 1918, they were married. When the National show closed at midnight, Bud and Betty, accompanied by a pair of other girls from the chorus, found an all-night club for a prewedding celebration, then drove to Alexandria, Virginia. They huddled together on the courthouse steps until the building opened, obtained a license, and were directed to the justice of the peace. Betty and the girls barely got back to the National in time for the matinee.

Bud and Betty settled down in a pleasant apartment which they could now afford with their combined salaries—$75 a week for him, $25 for her. Two weeks after the wedding, Bud arrived just before Betty was to leave for the matinee. She was surprised to see him, because he always went to the theater early and met her there.

"Did you forget something, darling?" she asked.

"No, I got bad news for you, baby," he said grimly.

"What is it?" she asked.

"We're canned, fired. No more show. The management is shutting down for an indefinite period. Something about salaries being too high for a profit."

"Oh, is that all?" Betty said lightly.

"Is that all? We're just married and now we're both out of work! I ain't saved a dime."

"I have." She smiled and he looked at her inquiringly. "Last year I had a Johnny, a banker who came every week to the show. Every week I got a box of candy, and I knew it came from him."

"How did you know?"

"He stared at me every time I was onstage. And down at the bottom of the candy was always a five- or ten-dollar gold piece. Well, he was a banker, wasn't he?"

"Did you go out with him?" Bud asked suspiciously.

"Once. But Billie Jackson went along with me—I insisted on that. All he wanted to do was take me out to dinner. That's the God's honest truth, Bud. And I never spent the gold pieces. I hid 'em under my lingerie. Here." She went to the chiffonier and extracted a handful of gleaming coins.

He stared at her dubiously, and she said, "All it was, was dinner. Ask Billie, she'll tell you." His face broke into a smile and he swept her into his arms.

They lived on the gold pieces until Bud was able to find a

Bud and Betty in one of their early routines

Harry Steppe and Bud

job. Not in show business this time; he became cashier at Harvey's Restaurant. It was a good job to have, since Bud could take his meals at work and bring home snacks for his bride. Both Bud and Betty grew restless, and they moved on to Cleveland, where he was hired as manager of the Empire Theater and she worked as soubrette and dancer. Bud was ambitious, and he believed he could produce shows of his own. He borrowed $1,500 from an uncle, a treasurer of Tammany Hall in New York, and staged Abbott's Revue. It did well on the Gus Sun circuit until it hit the small towns and ran out of customers. For three years Bud managed the National Theater in Detroit, staging a new show every week and thus absorbing an encyclopedia of burlesque routines. Rex Weber grew tired of being a feeder—a straight man who fed lines to his comic partner—and decided to become a comic himself. His distressing flaw was that he wasn't funny, and he was fired. "I can be a straight man," Bud decided.

The booker for the Hertigan-Seemans circuit was a friend of Bud's father, and he agreed to take a chance on the young straight man and his wife. Bud and Betty were hired on a three-year contract, and they developed a repertoire of comedy skits. The most successful was one in which Bud performed a number with chorus girls and expressed surprise when the audience laughed at their efforts. The laughter was caused by Betty, who was clowning behind them. For a closer she stood on her head and did the shimmy. It was surefire.

Those were joyous times for two young people in love with each other and show business. They learned to cherish the theatrical rooming houses like Mother's in Baltimore, where they could get three home-cooked meals a day and a room for $16 a week. Or the one operated by the three Buckley sisters in Philadelphia, where Bud and Betty were able to rent a room with the bathroom on the same floor instead of in the backyard. The Buckleys were kind-hearted spinsters who left midnight snacks on the dining room table for the performers to eat after the last show.

Traveling was a continual adventure. On the last day of an engagement, the performers packed their bags, checked out of the hotel, and took everything to the theater. As soon as the last show ended, they rushed to the station and boarded a train for the next date. They brought out the booze and talked about how well the Crazy House worked and what a bastard the theater manager had been. Then they uncovered the eats—ribs and fried chicken from a midnight diner, cookies and fruitcake mothers had sent from home. As the train rattled past darkened towns, the travelers at last folded down the seats and stretched out for sleep. Bud sat up all night playing poker. Bud drank in those years, too, but it was only the kind of drinking that performers needed to bring them down from the highs of working before audiences. Only once did Bud's boozing threaten his performance. Onstage in Montreal Betty noted that his ordinarily precise speech was slurred. Without dropping out of character, she snapped, "Why don't you talk straight," and his usual manner returned.

Playing Boston was always an adventure because of the censor. He insisted on a performance for himself alone, so he could protect his fellow citizens from impure entertainment. Bud and Betty's act was sly but scarcely suggestive, yet the censor found something he deemed objectionable. It was the following exchange:

Bud: "What's your name?"
Betty: "Pratt."
Bud: "Are you one of the Boston Pratts?"
Betty: "No, I'm just an ordinary Pratt."

Bud was able to retain the dialogue only by convincing the censor that Betty's name was indeed Pratt.

The only twinge of homesickness came at Christmastime when the burlesque people stared glumly out train windows at the lighted trees in houses they passed by. They made their own Christmas. Usually the theater was dark, so they could have an all-day celebration. A white sheet was spread on a hotel bed, and all the good things from home were laid out for a feast. Carols were sung around a tree, and everyone got presents, most of them small. Later, full of rum and sentiment, they ran down to the street and threw snowballs.

The traveling shows worked eight months a year, then

summer stock took over the burlesque houses. Performers who hadn't saved their money hoped to find work in vaudeville or cabarets or as tummelers (a combination M.C., comedian, and activities director) at hotels in the Catskills. The lucky ones spent their summers at Lake Hopatcong in New Jersey.

No one knew why burlesque people started coming there. It had become the oasis at the end of the long winter's travels, the place where comics and straight men rested beyond the reach of dunning hotel managers and mean-hearted theater owners, where strippers could eat their fill and not worry about diets until the last two weeks of summer. For the children it was heaven. During the year they had been entrusted to grandparents and aunts while the parents traveled. Now the family was reunited, and the kids could boat and swim and bask in the hot New Jersey sun and at night stage precocious entertainments with tablecloths as costumes and makeup borrowed from their parents. Bud tried to save $500 during the year, or he borrowed from the average citizen's moneylender, the Morris Plan. He rented a cottage and a boat and on Saturday nights he and Betty joined the other burlesque people at Glasser's Restaurant to dine and talk over prospects for the coming season.

Summers at the lake reunited the Abbott family. Rae Abbott, who lived with Bud and Betty much of the time after her husband died, came there, as well as Harry, Jr., who ran the Corinthian Theater in Rochester. Also there were Olive, who had worked in the chorus, married, and had two children, Norman and Betty, and Babe, who had been talking woman—female equivalent of straight man—with such performers as Walter Huston and Billy Gilbert. Another family member in burlesque was Al Golden, Bud's first cousin and generally acknowledged as the best straight man in the business. Bud listened closely to his cousin's instructions, and he applied the lessons when he went back to burlesque after the summer's respite. He learned to read the moods and movements of the comics he worked with. Some were dullards who repeated the funny stuff by rote, never experiencing the thrill of lifting an audience to a new level of enjoyment. Some were inspired improvisationists, sensing an

36

audience's mood and playing it with variations, like a Bach fugue. Some were manic, performing three feet off the stage floor with a holiday crowd; others were depressive, sparse audiences sending them into fits of unfunniness. Bud could deal with either range. Like all straight men, he gave close attention to his appearance, his elegant clothes offering sharp contrast to the outrageous getups of the comics. Bud was considered a comer by his fellow burlesque performers, who reckoned that a good straight man was worth three comics (the straight man was usually billed first in a comedy team).

Bud joined with Harry Steppe, a funny Jewish comic but one subject to spells of melancholia. Another partner was Harry Evanson, an inventive man whose small thin frame offered an amusing contrast to the tall Bud. With both Steppe and Evanson, Bud had the uncommon knack of making them seem funnier than they were. His style is evident even in the publicity photos from his early years in burlesque. The hair slicked back over his high forehead. The smiling eyes and winning grin. Straw hat and striped pants, dark jacket and vest, silk hankie folded casually in the breast pocket, silk carnation in the lapel. The tie knotted tightly around the starched collar, jeweled links on the French cuffs, jeweled ring on the pinkie. Feet in polished black-and-whites planted confidently apart. There is the impression that what he wore underneath was all silk.

Everyone in burlesque agreed that Bud Abbott would go far, if he could only find the right comic to team up with.

4

Lou Costello:
The Early Years

HE WAS BAPTIZED Louis Francis Cristillo, and he was a fat, bright, alert baby who grew into an ambitious young man. Reared in an immigrant community of New Jersey, he was instilled with the American success story. He wanted to be loved, enjoyed, acclaimed. There could be no more fulfilling way of achieving that than to be a movie star. He studied Charlie Chaplin with worshipful envy. Everyone talked of the little tramp, everyone adored him. The chubby boy tried to put himself into the spare frame of the English comic. Lou saw *Shoulder Arms* twenty-five times, until he could repeat every scene, every gesture.

Lou was three-quarters Italian and one-quarter Irish, which may help to explain his volatility, his outgoing charm, the blackness of his moods. His paternal grandfather was captain of the carabinieri in a village near Naples, a stern man who decreed that his son would become a priest. But Sebastian Cristillo was too attached to the mortal world, and he left the seminary to join a brother who had emigrated to Paterson, New Jersey. Philip Cristillo worked as a weaver and he got his brother a job at the mill and began teaching him English, a language that Sebastian never quite mastered. Sebastian found mill work boring and he was happy to acquire a position with the Singer Sewing Machine Company driving a horse and wagon to make

38

deliveries and repairs. When his English improved, he managed to get hired by the Prudential Insurance Company as a salesman.

Sebastian fell in love with an Irish-Italian girl, Helen Rege, and they were married on New Year's Day, 1902, and moved in with her family at 14 Madison Street. On December 10 of that year Helen Cristillo gave birth to a son, who was named Anthony Sebastian. A second son, named Louis Francis after Helen's father, was born on March 6, 1906, and a daughter, Marie Teresa, on December 11, 1911. The Cristillo children grew up in a warm, crowded, profoundly Italian home which was shared by their grandfather, Uncle Pete, Aunt Alma, Aunt May, and Aunt Eva. The house also served as a way station for Italian immigrants; arrivals at Ellis Island passed the word along that a nice woman in Paterson named Helen Cristillo would help them to understand English and to get a start in the new land. As Sebastian's fortunes improved, he moved everyone to a two-family house at 106 East 33rd Street in a better part of town.

Helen Cristillo had many fine qualities, but the art of cooking eluded her. Sebastian prepared dinners, conjuring up aromatic dishes learned from his mother in Italy. The Cristillo children always looked forward to Friday, because that was when he made pasta fazule; all week long he collected leftover pasta and soaked it in bean water along with olive oil and chunks of stale bread. Sebastian played the mandolin and he insisted that Anthony learn the violin, despite Anthony's complaints about the hazards of carrying a violin case through tough neighborhoods to his lessons. His father was convinced the boy would become a virtuoso. After a teacher disciplined Anthony by rapping his knuckles, Sebastian stormed into the classroom and admonished, "You wanna hit, you hit. But never hitta de hands!" He had musical ambitions for Lou as well and made the boy study piano, trumpet, and drums, but the lessons didn't take. Helen Cristillo saw to her children's spiritual training, insisting that they attend Mass every Sunday. She herself prayed other days as well, not necessarily at the Catholic church. Some days she went to the synagogue: "It's closer to home, and I can pray there just as well," she explained.

At P.S. 15 Lou was a reluctant student, more interested in pranks and athletics than in studying. He was a superior basketball player, three times winning the New Jersey championship for free-throwing. He was good at baseball and boxing, too. The entertainment world fascinated him. He haunted the Paterson vaudeville and movie houses. He and his brother played hooky to see *The Covered Wagon,* and when the lights came on in the theater, their father was seated behind them. A lover of movie westerns, Sebastian Cristillo nevertheless paddled his sons when they got home.

Lou attended high school only during basketball season. But despite his skill as a shooter, he realized he could never become a star at the sport because of his size—five feet, four inches. He had tried prizefighting and had decided after fourteen bouts that the punishments were not worth the rewards. Vaudeville was the answer to his search for recognition. He devised an act patterned transparently after his idol, Charlie Chaplin, and he tried it out before vaudeville agents, smoking a cigar to make himself seem older. Neither the act nor the cigar made an impression.

Anthony Cristillo, the older son, had left home to join the Navy during the war, became weary of swabbing decks, and volunteered for the ship orchestra. Discharged in 1921, he went into the music business in New York, was given a new first name by a girlfriend ("I'll call you 'Pat' because you're from Paterson"). He became leader of his own band. Cristillo was not easy to remember, so he took the name of the acting family, Costello. When Lou started his own acting career, he followed his brother's example.

Papa Cristillo could not understand why his first-born needed to abandon his family name, nor did he approve of Tony's choice of occupation. Although he adored music, he did not comprehend how his son could make a living from playing dance music in New York hotels. Sebastian would have been much happier if Tony (now Pat) had continued with his schooling and found steady work as a bookkeeper or a pharmacist.

And then one evening Lou announced that he was leaving home.

"And where do you thinka you're going?" his father asked.

"To Hollywood," Lou replied resolutely.

"To-a *Holly*wood!" his father exclaimed. "Whacha wanna do dat for? Doncha know dey got Indians out there?"

"Now, Pop, you been seein' too many western movies. The only Indians they got out there are in front of cigar stores."

"No, no, no, I donna like it. First your brudder go 'way to be a sailor-boy an' he come back with a different name I never heard before."

Pat was home on a visit, and he interjected, "I told you, Pop, nobody is going to buy 'Anthony Sebastian Cristillo and his dance band.'"

"So now you're Pat Costello. I don't know that name. You lemme talk to Lou. Whassa matter with Paterson, Lou? Why can't you finish your school and find a nice-a job in the grocery store or maybe worka department store."

"I ain't gonna be no floorwalker, Pop," Lou insisted. "I'm gonna go out to Hollywood and become a movie star. I know I can do it."

Papa Cristillo shook his head sadly. "I donna understan'. In the old country, only the richa kids, dey can go to school. Here, everybody canna go to school, but my two sons, they no wanna. Why?"

"I told you, Pop. What I want, you can't get in school."

"I don' like it," said Lou's father.

"Look, Pop," Pat said, "if you don't let him go and he ends up a bum, he'll always blame you. Let him go. I'm working now. If Lou needs some dough in California, I'll send it to him."

Helen Cristillo remained neutral in the argument, realizing her son's devotion to his dream but unwilling to oppose her husband's will. In the end, Sebastian relented. He not only permitted Lou to depart for Hollywood, he managed to find $200 for his son's journey.

Lou had a companion for his western trek. He was a Paterson schoolmate, Gene Coogan, and together they made their way across the country, hitchhiking with motorists or climbing aboard freight trains. They arrived in Los Angeles on a summery day in 1927, and Lou was more than ever convinced of the wisdom of his trip. The wide, palm-lined avenues, the squat, white stucco bungalows, the sunswept gardens seemed enormously attractive after urban New Jersey. Lou and Gene rented a room with their remaining funds and began exploring the city. A nickle or a dime on the Pacific Electric could take them along Sunset Boulevard, where the ruins of D. W. Griffith's Babylon were still standing; to Poverty Row, where authentic cowboys in chaps and ten-gallon hats waited for studio jobs; to Universal City, where a small fee allowed a grandstand view of movies being made.

There was much to excite a movie-struck kid in 1926 Hollywood. Lou could dream of being invited to Pickfair, where Douglas Fairbanks and Mary Pickford ruled benignly as king and queen of equal status. Bill Hart and Theda Bara had faded, but there were newcomers who had even greater promise as stars: Greta Garbo, Gary Cooper, Janet Gaynor, Buddy Rogers, Fay Wray, Dolores Del Rio. Almost every week brought premieres of big pictures like *Ben-Hur, Beau Geste, Son of the Sheik, Old Ironsides,* and *The Black Pirate,* and Lou watched the stars arrive in their Duesenbergs and Pierce-Arrows. He yearned to be on the other side of the rope. But how? He was just a raw kid from New Jersey, good-looking and athletic but hardly a Richard Dix, too short to be a leading man.

He believed he could succeed in comedy. Everyone in school had always said how funny he was, although his teachers were not always amused. Lou adored the comedies of Charlie Chaplin, Harold Lloyd, Harry Langdon, and Buster Keaton. He wanted to be like them.

Neither Lou nor Gene Coogan found any encouragement at the studios. Their money dwindled, and Lou was too proud to write home and admit his failure in Hollywood. During the summer he lived on fruit he stole at night from neighborhood orchards. Always a voracious eater, he stifled his appetite by subsisting on cheap candy. He and Coogan rented a room but could not afford blankets; on cold nights they slept between the mattresses. When the landlord evicted them for nonpayment of rent, the pair slept in cars they found parked on streets and in car lots. Lou awoke before dawn, for a three-hour walk to a distant studio.

He concentrated his efforts on Metro-Goldwyn-Mayer. Louis B. Mayer and Irving Thalberg had gathered the movie industry's largest array of stars, and Lou was certain that the studio would find room for him. Finally it did.

"I got a job! I got a job!" he announced to Gene Coogan when they met in the evening to hunt for a car suitable for sleeping.

"Gee, that's great, Lou!" his friend replied. "Where?"

"M-G-M, of course. Nothin' but the best for me."

"What kind of a part is it?"

"Well, it's not exactly a part."

"What is it?"

"I'm gonna be a carpenter an' build sets. But I'll be around where they're making movies, and I'll betcha one of those directors at M-G-M is gonna discover me."

It didn't happen as Lou had predicted. Lou drifted away from the work gang to visit sets where Norma Shearer and Ramon Novarro were appearing in *The Student Prince*, Marie Dressler and Polly Moran in *The Callahans and the Murphys*. But no director ever noticed him.

One day Lou wandered out to Lot 2, where one of his idols, John Gilbert, was appearing in a swashbuckler, *Bardelys the Magnificent*. The director, King Vidor, was contemplating a scene in which a victim of Gilbert's swordsmanship would fall off the top of a 30-foot building.

"We'll have to get a stunt man," Vidor said to his assistant, "and we'll need to replace that gravel with sand to cushion the fall. We're going to lose some time."

"I'll do it, Mr. Vidor," Lou volunteered.

The director turned around and noticed the eager-faced carpenter.

"I heard what you said," Lou continued. "I can do that stunt and you won't lose any time."

"I don't think it's safe," Vidor replied. "We need to dig up that ground and make it softer."

"I can do it! Watch me."

Before Vidor could protest, Lou climbed to the top of the building and flung himself from the roof. He landed with a thud that made Vidor and the set workers wince. But Lou rose to his feet and said, "Okay?"

"Okay," the director agreed. "If you're crazy enough to do it again, I'll hire you."

Lou Costello became the busiest and most daring stunt man at M-G-M. His compact size made him ideal for doubling for female stars, and he took falls for Dolores Del Rio in *The Trail of '98* and Joan Crawford in *Taxi Dancer*. The end of his career came when he impersonated William Haines in a football picture. The first-string varsity of the University of Southern California landed on him, and Lou ended up in the hospital. His bones healed, but he realized he had pushed his luck as a stunt man. The film industry was in a jumble because of the conversion to talkies, and no other work was available. Lou began a new diet of bread and jam for three meals a day. He sent a pleading letter to his brother, but Pat was traveling with his orchestra and didn't receive it. Finally Lou and Gene Coogan gave up. Dejectedly they started for home.

Their return was even more haphazard than the western journey. Lou and Gene begged for nickels on street corners. They slept in boxcars and barns. They worked on a Colorado farm during the wheat harvest. They reached their lowest ebb in Kansas. Struggling along a country road exhausted from hunger, they approached a pasture of cows. Lou had never milked a cow before, but he had seen it done in movies. He climbed the fence, found a preoccupied donor, filled the cup he carried with him. The nourishment allowed Lou and Gene to press on to Topeka.

"I got some relatives in Lawrence, Kansas," Gene remarked. "If we could just get there, I know they'd put us up for a while."

"Yeah, but how're we gonna get there?" Lou asked. "My legs feel like stumps."

"We gotta get some dough for a bus ride. Got any ideas?"

"Fresh out."

They were walking along the streets of Topeka in the warm afternoon when they came to a burlesque theater. "GIRLS! GIRLS! GIRLS!" the marquee advertised. "BIG BEAUTY CHORUS— CONTINUOUS SHOW—COMEDIANS, SCENERY, AND SPECIALTY ACTS —NEW SHOW EVERY FRIDAY."

"That's it!" Lou said excitedly.

"What're you talking about?" Gene said. "We don't have any money for the burleycue."

"No, dummy, we'll get jobs in the show. Or at least a handout. Show people are a soft touch. C'mon, let's find the stage door. And let me do the talkin'."

Lou bluffed his way past the doorman and found the stage manager in his tiny office. "How do you do, I'm Lou Costello and this is my friend, Gene Coogan," Lou said rapidly. "We been out in Hollywood makin' pictures and now we're going back to New York for an engagement. Meanwhile we're a bit short of cash and wondered if you could use a couple of actors for a week or two."

The manager eyed the two ragged young men and replied, "No openings."

"Well, then, do you know of any other opportunities for actors with Hollywood experience?"

"I know the burlesque house in St. Jo is looking for a Dutch comic."

"Great! One other thing."

"What's that?"

"Could you lend us five bucks to get there?"

The five dollars got Lou and Gene only as far as Lawrence, where Gene's relatives provided food and shelter for the road-weary travelers. Lou telephoned St. Joseph and confirmed that the burlesque theater needed a Dutch comic. Lou said he would arrive there shortly to assume the position.

"But you've never been on a stage," Gene reminded him.

"Whassa difference?" Lou replied. "I'm a funny guy, ain't I?"

"Yeah, you're funny. But you ain't Dutch."

"But I can talk Dutch, or German or Jewish or any other goddam accent. I heard 'em all in Paterson."

The theater in St. Joseph was desperate enough for a comic that it hired the inexperienced young man. He learned fast, soaking up all the expertise of comics and straight men who had been in the profession since the turn of the century. Lou's impish face and lively manner soon made him a favorite in St. Joseph, especially with the town whores. They brought their customers and sat in boxes overlooking the stage.

Lou moved on to a St. Louis theater and was so well received that he wanted to share his triumph with his family. Papa and Mama Cristillo, Pat and his sister Marie took the train west for a joyful reunion with Lou. The family went to the theater to see Lou on the stage for the first time. Sebastian laughed until tears streamed down his ruddy cheeks. Helen was enormously proud of her younger son, but she couldn't avoid asking him, "Why do those young ladies have to take off their clothes?"

And so Lou Costello continued his travels through Depression America, learning his trade. Millions were jobless but Lou never missed a week's work. His reputation as a funny young man preceded him along the circuit, and theater managers welcomed him for three-week or four-week engagements—or longer.

Among the many things Lou enjoyed about burlesque was the proximity of the chorus girls. In 1934 he was playing a small theater in New York when he became attracted to a pretty dancer named Anne Battler, who had come to America from Scotland at eleven and had grown up in South Attleboro, Massachusetts. Lou claimed later that he tried to wangle an introduction to Anne and failed. Friends told her of the young comic's interest and one day she watched him rehearse a sketch. He lurched off stage, bounced against a hall tree that hit her on the head. "Gee, I'm sorry," Lou said as she lay dazed on the floor. She agreed to his offer to go to the delicatessen for a sandwich. Four months later they were married.

Lou blossomed in burlesque. After the starvation in California, he ate his fill in every city. Hot dogs and ice cream were his favorites; he could down a dozen dogs and a quart of ice cream at one sitting. His comedic skill seemed to grow with his waistline, a little fat guy being funnier than a little thin guy. Lou watched the other comics, studied how they could milk a laugh by rotating their hands in their trouser pockets or by growling doglike at top-heavy talking women. But Lou was not an imitator. He knew that he would have to develop his own style if he were to accomplish his ambition: to return to Hollywood as a star.

5

The Partnership Begins

DERBY TILTED back on his head, Bud Abbott leaned on his ivory-handled cane. He stood in the wings of the Eltinge Theater in New York, studying the events onstage with the cool assessment of a trader viewing the quotation board at the stock exchange. There was a new comic in town, a fat little guy named Lou Costello, and Bud had been hearing about him for months. They were good reports mostly, although some of the older straight men claimed Costello was inclined to go wild. Bud watched him closely.

It was the Lemon Table Routine. Costello was the sucker who was confident he could pick which of the three coconut half-shells contained the lemon. Joe Lyons played the straight man, sliding the three shells over the table until the lemon dropped in the basket below, unbeknownst to the sucker. He displayed the empty cup where the lemon had been and collected the bet. Lyons didn't have the finesse, Bud realized. His gab wasn't smooth enough to be a street pitchman, and he had no dexterity with the shells. Bud had done the Lemon Table a thousand times, and he made the cup-switching a ballet. It was the most important element of the routine, motivating the sucker's confusion over the location of the lemon. Joe Lyons simply wasn't doing it right.

But the Costello kid was all right. Damn good, in fact, even

The first known photograph together, 1936

The Lemon Table Routine, a classic bit in burlesque

CREDIT: FANCHON & MARCO

CREDIT: JACK PARTINGTON, JR.

without a strong straight man. He had the audience with him. Each time he wailed when he couldn't find the lemon, the audience roared with understanding amusement. The little guy moved well, not like some of the fat comics who stood like monuments on the stage. And when he turned the table on the pitchman and tried the lemon switch himself, his ineptitude was quite marvelous.

"Hi, I'm Bud Abbott."

The sweaty little man in the droopy pants looked up at the smartly dressed figure. "Yeah, I hearda you," Lou replied. He patted the rear of the last chorus girl in the line that was filing onstage for the finale.

"I've heard of you, too," Bud replied. "I liked what you do with the Lemon Table. Reminds me of Joe Yule."

"Bullshit. I never seen Joe Yule. An' I don't steal from nobody."

"I didn't say you stole anything. I was just giving you a compliment."

"Okay, I accept."

For weeks they played on the same bill at the Eltinge, Lou with Joe Lyons, Bud with Harry Evanson. Bud continued studying the fat little comic from New Jersey. When he was onstage with Evanson, Bud sometimes caught a glimpse of Costello standing by the curtain and watching him.

Bud and Lou became better acquainted, and so did their wives. Betty still worked with Bud as talking woman, but Anne was pregnant and had left burlesque. One Saturday night Lou suggested that the Abbotts and Costellos meet for supper after the midnight show.

They went to Reuben's, and Bud ordered a double scotch and Lou two Reuben sandwiches. While the two wives talked about backstage gossip, Lou blurted, "I think we oughta work together."

"You do, huh?" Bud replied.

"Yeah, Joe Lyons is okay, but he don't have no style. You got style."

"Thanks."

50

"So how about it. Interested?"

"Yes, I'm interested. Matter of fact, I've been having problems with Harry. He's a funny guy but moody. He's starting to drink before the shows, and you notice that's something I never do."

"I noticed," Lou answered.

"Yes, I'm interested," Bud repeated.

"And?" Lou asked.

"And what?"

"And whadya got to say about me? You think I'm funny?"

"Yes, you're funny. I think you've got a real future."

"It took you a long time to say it."

"Of course you need the right kind of handling. You go a little wild sometimes."

"But it's funny, ain't it?"

"Sometimes. Not always. If we teamed up, I'd want to be sure you'd listen to me."

"I'll listen. Honest to God, I will," Lou promised. "You been in burlesque longer than me. I respect your experience. You wanna try it together?"

"Sure. Why not?"

"Hey—great!" Lou's shout brought the attention of Betty and Anne, as well as other patrons of Reuben's. "Ladies, I want you to meet the new stars of burlesque," Lou announced. "Costello and Abbott!"

Bud shook his head. "You know the straight man always goes first. It's 'Abbott and Costello.'"

Lou shrugged assent. "I'm going on the road next week," he said, "but I'll be back in a month. Don't make no plans until I get back—okay?"

"Okay, partner," Bud smiled.

"Let me go! Let me go!" Lou would cry when they returned to the dressing room. "I start getting hot and you pull me back. Don't interrupt me. Let me go."

"Naw," Bud would answer. "You get carried away. You'll lose 'em if you go too far."

It is always so, this mystic relation between comic and straight man. Even the best of comics—Bobby Clark, Bert Lahr, Red Skelton, Jerry Lewis—could go too far and exhaust and ultimately bore the audience. Lou was in danger of doing that, too. Bud realized it, and he always applied the restraining hand. Let Lou go so far and then bring him back. Let him go wild but finally slap him on the shoulder and say, "Talk sense!" Get him back on the track before he derails the whole sketch. That was the straight man's genius. His detractors claimed, "Bud fell in the toilet when he met Lou and came up covered with gold." Not so. Theirs was an equal partnership, though few people realized it. Not even Bud and Lou.

They worked for Minsky in New York and played the road circuit, drawing from the comic literature of burlesque, expanding here, cutting there, honing each sketch to perfection. In its search for survival, burlesque was getting dirtier, the strippers whipping themselves into orgiastic frenzies, and the comics aiming their shticks below the belt. Bud and Lou wouldn't play dirty. Something in their backgrounds wouldn't allow them to try for the smutty laugh. They didn't need to. Why aim at the crotch when so many belly laughs could be found in the burlesque bits? They were a curious blend, totally devoid of the sophistication of sketches in vaudeville and Broadway revues. Burlesque comedy was peopled with common citizens: cops and compliant females, grifters and bumpkins. Judges, politicos, and other figures of authority were the objects of ridicule, and triumph over the sucker was celebrated. If the country cousin didn't get fleeced of his bankroll, then he got beaten with bladders and drowned in seltzer.

Despite their travels, Bud and Lou remained close to their families. After Anne gave birth to her first daughter, Patricia, in 1937, the Costellos gave up their New York apartment and made their home with the Costello parents in Paterson. Whenever Lou came off the road, he hurried back to Paterson for a reunion with Anne and the baby, with his parents and the rest of the family.

The center for the Abbott family was the Coolidge Hotel

in New York City. The hotel was on 47th Street, once called "The Street of Dreams" by O. Henry but later termed "Malaria Alley" by Walter Winchell. The Coolidge Hotel, with its faded charm and substandard rates, became a mecca for burlesque people. Pimps, prostitutes, and purse snatchers frequented 47th Street, but the burlesque performers and their children were safe. The taxi drivers acted as protective knights, warning suspicious characters not to molest the inhabitants of the Coolidge Hotel.

Bud had a secret, and it remained unknown except to a handful of intimates for his entire life. He was an epileptic.

Bud and Betty had been married eight years before the first seizure came. Thereafter the epilepsy returned with terrifying unpredictability. Lou was surprised and frightened when he witnessed an attack for the first time. He learned that Bud would come out of a seizure very quickly after it began. The tell-tale sign came when Bud started to veer sideways. Lou then aimed a hard blow at Bud's gut. The hit to the solar plexus always seemed a part of the harum-scarum of their routine, and the audiences responded with laughter, never realizing that the blow had forestalled a ghastly scene. Norman Abbott, who often accompanied his uncle on engagements, always carried a supply of pencils in his pocket; whenever Bud felt a fit coming, he asked Norman for a pencil to jam in his mouth to prevent biting his tongue.

Norman adored his uncle just as Bud had idolized his older brother Harry. The boy was upset when he saw Bud drink too much. "Why, Bud? Why?" Norman asked. Bud told him why. Bud had sought the advice of the best doctors, and they had told him that the epilepsy could not be cured. Scotch became Bud's companion in his escape from fear of seizures in the night. Even so, he always kept a pencil on the bedside table, in case a seizure should come.

The new team of Abbott and Costello found favor with patrons of the burlesque houses, and their vogue might have flourished and wilted in that specialized arena of entertainment.

To escape such a fate they needed a zealot who would devote his life to their success. It turned out to be Eddie Sherman. Originally he was called Itzchok Ussishkin, and he was the son of a kosher butcher and grandson of a rabbi. They lived in the village of Meshabesh, 200 miles from Odessa, at a time when life in Russia was becoming unpleasant for Jews. The grandfather left for Palestine, borrowed the name of Plesser, and helped found Israel. His son bought a passport with the name of Sherman and moved his wife and seven children to South Philadelphia. The year was 1914, and Itzchok was eleven and newly named Edward. He had only been to Hebrew school and knew no English, so he started in the first grade; within three years he had graduated from grammar school. Six months at Central High School convinced him to try the outer world, and he quit to work in a drugstore. Singing alto in temple drew him toward show business and soon he was working in the Yiddish theater, playing bit parts and supplying scripts for plays that had never been written down before; nobody had ever provided "sides"—sheets containing the lines and cues for a single role—for the actors to study. He found a cache of playlet scripts in the theater, translated them into English, and sold them to the vaudeville house across the street. Young Eddie realized he was better at dealing than acting, and soon he had a thriving business as a talent booker for vaudeville and movie theaters in Pennsylvania and New Jersey.

A talent booker hates nothing more than empty stages. Eddie Sherman found such a situation at the Atlantic City Steel Pier, which was being operated by a former Buick salesman. Eddie convinced him to try a vaudeville show with the assurance that the talent could be booked for $300 a week. Within three months the Steel Pier was expending $30,000 a week for talent in its three big showplaces. Eddie Cantor, Harry Richman, and George Jessel appeared on a single bill; the bands of Jimmy Dorsey, Guy Lombardo, and Tommy Dorsey alternated in the ballroom; circuses and minstrel shows attracted the summer throngs. When the Pier owner balked at paying $3,500 for a weekend appearance of Amos 'n' Andy, Eddie talked them into chancing a 50–50 split. They played eleven shows on Saturday and thirteen on Sunday and walked off with $23,000.

Frank Elliott, who produced the minstrel show at the Steel Pier, told Eddie Sherman that he needed a couple of comics for the summer season. "I'll look around," said Eddie with certainty. He was spending two days a week at the New York offices of the William Morris Agency, where he shared quarters with the vaudeville booker, Johnny Hyde. One day Louis Epstein, manager of Al Jolson, came by for a visit.

"I saw a couple of great comics at the burlesque house over on 46th Street," said Epstein. "You oughta go look at them."

Eddie Sherman did, and he was suitably impressed. The straight man was tall and thin, wore clothes well and had a sure delivery. The comic was short and fat, with a little-boy look that made him all the more sympathetic when he absorbed the beatings on Floogle Street. Sherman brought the minstrel show producer, Frank Elliott, to see the burlesque comics. Elliott agreed that they were good; what was more, their act was clean enough to appeal to the family audiences of the Steel Pier. He offered a contract for ten summer weeks at $150 a week for the pair. When Eddie presented the deal to Bud and Lou, he drew a mixed reception.

Bud, eleven years older than Lou and more experienced in the show world, responded first. "It's too risky," he said. "We're already getting a hundred and fifty in burlesque and we're guaranteed forty weeks a year. Why the hell should we give that up to play some goddam minstrel show for ten weeks?"

"What are you talking about, Abbott?" Lou said. "You wanna stay in burlesque all your life?"

"What's wrong with that?"

"Well, I ain't gonna spend the rest of my life following strippers, I'll tell you that. This is our chance to break out, Bud, to get into the big time."

"You call a minstrel show on a pier big time?"

Eddie Sherman exerted his own quiet but considerable

powers of persuasion, arguing a bright future for the team in other realms of entertainment. Bud was unmoved.

"I've slept in too many fleabags to start all over again," Bud said. "What happens when summer is over? We'll be lucky to find a job."

Lou now played his trump card. "I want this date," he said. "I want it so bad I'm willing to let you have eighty-five dollars of the hundred fifty, and I'll take sixty-five."

Bud stared at him in astonishment. "You'd do that?"

"I said I would."

"Okay, we'll take it," Bud told Eddie Sherman. "But I think we're making a big mistake." Indeed it was a mistake, as Bud would discover four years later.

6

From the Steel Pier
to *The Kate Smith Hour*

"GENTLEMEN, be seated...."

Amid a fluttering of tambourines, the thirty black-faced entertainers took their chairs onstage, elegantly parting the tails of their milk-white costumes as they sat down. The interlocutor began immediately by posing straight lines to the end men, who responded with ancient jokes. Mr. Bones did an eccentric tap dance, and a trio sang a medley of Stephen Foster tunes.

"And now, ladies and gentlemen, I want you to give a warm Atlantic City welcome to the newest members of our jolly band of merrymakers—Mr. Bud Abbott and Mr. Lou Costello."

The applause was warm but not overwhelming as Bud and Lou, their faces blackened with cork, stepped down from the platform and walked to center-stage. They launched into one of their routines.

Bud: Didn't I see you at the race track yesterday?

Lou: Yeah, I was there. I like to bet on the nags.

Bud (grabbing him): Don't talk like that about horses! Do you realize that I have one of the greatest mudders in the country?

Lou: What has your mother got to do with horses?

Bud: My mudder *is* a horse.

Lou: What? I will admit there's a resemblance.

Bud: Now stop that!

Lou: Is your mudder really a horse?

Bud: Of course. My mudder won the first race at Hialeah yesterday.

Lou: You oughta be ashamed of yourself, putting your mudder in a horse race.

Bud: What are you talking about? My mudder used to pull a milk wagon.

Lou: What some people won't do for a living!

Bud: I take very good care of my mudder. If she don't feel like running, I scratch my mudder.

Lou: Now ain't that cozy! I suppose if you get an itch your mudder scratches you.

Bud: You don't follow me.

Lou: Not when you're related to a bunch of horses, I don't. I won't even *speak* to you.

Bud: Will you make sense? I said I've got a fine horse and he's a mudder.

Lou (astounded): *He's* a mudder! How can *he* be a mudder?

Bud: Because *he* makes a better mudder than a *she*. Now I can't waste my time with you. I've got to go to the track and feed my mudder.

Lou: And what do you give the old lady for breakfast—oats?

Bud: Don't be old-fashioned. Modern mudders don't eat oats. They eat their fodder.

Lou: What did you say?

Bud: I said I feed my mudder his fodder.

Lou: What have you got—a bunch of cannibals? . . .

At every show the Abbott and Costello routines brought waves of laughter from the Steel Pier vacationers, confirming Eddie Sherman's belief in the team's future. If their burlesque routines remained surefire when delivered in blackface at a minstrel show, they could succeed in any medium—radio, the Broadway theater, cabarets, movies. At the end of the Steel Pier engagement in the summer of 1937, Sherman came to the dressing room.

"What are you guys going to do next?" Sherman asked.

"Go back to burlesque, of course," Bud replied.

"I got a better idea," said Sherman.

"What's that?" Lou asked.

"I think you would be taking a step backward by going back to burlesque," Sherman said.

"What are you talking about?" Bud snapped. "Burlesque has been good to Lou and me."

"Shut up a minute and listen to the little man," Lou told Bud.

"Burlesque is on the skids; it's going the way of vaudeville," Sherman said.

"Bullshit!" Bud said. "We can still get forty weeks of bookings."

"*This* year," Sherman said. "Look what La Guardia did in New York; he padlocked the burlesque houses. Bluenoses all over the country are going to try the same. And besides, you wanta play in skid-row theaters all your lives?"

"What's your suggestion?" Lou asked.

"I think I can get you bookings in movie houses. Night clubs, too," Sherman said.

"Radio? Pictures?" Lou asked.

"Eventually," Sherman said. "I'd like to represent you boys. That means I'd make the deals."

"And we'd pay you ten percent," Bud suggested.

"That's right," said Sherman. "I don't work for nothing."

"I think we oughta go with the little man," Lou said. "I'd rather have ninety percent of some real dough than a hunnert percent of the chickenshit we've been getting."

And so Bud and Lou agreed to engage Eddie Sherman as their manager. In the first months it appeared that Bud's fears had been warranted. He and Lou were paid $20 for a day at Willow Grove Park, Philadelphia; $65 for three days at the State Theater in Baltimore; $125 a week at the Carman Theater in Philadelphia. Patience, Eddie Sherman counseled; these things take time to build. He pointed to a hopeful sign—each theater that booked Bud and Lou wanted them back, always at higher pay. And the theater managers were always surprised that the

With the great Kate Smith

*Onstage with Ted Collins,
the man who didn't think
"Who's on First?"
would get a laugh*

pair never repeated their material, unlike the vaudevillians who had little repertoire to draw from. The checks got bigger, $175 for a week at Fay's Theater in Philly, $300 for the Hippodrome in Baltimore. Then at last the big break, the Loew's State in New York. Eddie Sherman calculated that it was time to push Bud and Lou beyond playing stage shows in movie houses. He needed the help of a big agency, and he urged his friends at the William Morris Agency to catch Bud and Lou's act at Loew's State. They did, and the William Morris office became agents for Bud and Lou. The president of the company, Abe Lastfogel, assigned an energetic, dedicated young agent, Sam Weisbord, to work with the new clients.

Weisbord charted his strategy. He needed to expose Abbott and Costello to a mass audience, and the quickest way to do that was in radio. In the late 1930s, the networks were competing fiercely as advertisers realized the efficiency of radio in selling products. General Motors, Ford, Standard Brands, Procter & Gamble, Liggett and Myers, American Tobacco, and other huge corporations were pouring millions into sponsorship to capture the purchasing power freed by the end of the Depression. Burns and Allen, Major Bowes, Fred Allen, Eddie Cantor, Bob Hope, Stoopnagle and Budd, Jack Benny, Phil Baker, Edgar Bergen and Charlie McCarthy, Fibber McGee and Molly became national favorites, and their radio popularity enhanced their earning capacities in motion pictures, personal appearances, and other fields.

The National Broadcasting Company remained preeminent with its two networks, the Red and the Blue. The Columbia Broadcasting System, headed by William Paley, was struggling to compete. A prime time slot was Thursday at 9, which had long been dominated by *The Rudy Vallee Hour* on NBC. Paley tried to compete with an expensive production starring Kate Smith and produced by her mentor, Ted Collins. *The Kate Smith Hour* had failed to match Vallee's ratings, and Sam Weisbord calculated that Collins would be the likeliest producer to consider new talent.

"Ted, I've got a great new act," Weisbord told Collins.

"Their names are Abbott and Costello and they're right out of burlesque—"

"Are you kidding?" Collins interrupted. "Do you think I can put burlesque comedy on radio—with Kate?"

"No, no, they're not dirty. Even in burlesque they played it clean. They were a sensation at the Loew's State."

"What kind of stuff do they do?"

"You know—burlesque routines. Surefire stuff."

"They sound pretty visual for radio."

"They *are* visual, but they're great on dialogue, too. I'd like you to hear them, then decide for yourself."

Collins agreed. Weisbord brought Bud and Lou to the producer's office, and the pair performed the Racetrack Routine. Collins received the performance with a straight face. "It's funny," he conceded, "but it's too visual. The folks at home won't understand what is going on."

"You're wrong, Ted," Weisbord insisted. "You could have closed your eyes and gotten the same effect. I'll tell you this: these boys are going to be big stars. Now you wouldn't want to go down in history as the man who turned down Abbott and Costello, would you, Ted?"

Weisbord had employed the fear technique, and it worked. Collins agreed to hire Bud and Lou for a single performance at $350. The appearance was well received, although there were complaints that listeners couldn't tell Bud's voice from Lou's. Collins agreed to a return performance, and this time Lou raised his voice to a higher pitch, providing the little-boy quality that made him more appealing.

Collins kept asking Bud and Lou to return, and each Monday the producer auditioned a new routine. One day Bud and Lou offered the Baseball Routine. Collins sat through it without a trace of a smile. "Not funny," Collins commented when they finished. "Let's try something else."

"The guy's crazy," Lou said afterward. "The Baseball Routine has never failed. You know that."

"Of course I know that," Bud said. "But what are we going to do? He's the boss."

A few weeks later they tried a gambit on Collins. On Monday Lou told him that they didn't have a routine ready. Lou reported the same on Tuesday and Wednesday. "Maybe we better skip a week," Lou suggested.

"Absolutely not," Collins said emphatically, aware that ratings for *The Kate Smith Hour* had ascended since Abbott and Costello joined the cast. "I guess you'll have to do that silly baseball number. Maybe it won't be too bad."

The response to "Who's on First?" was enormous—a record number of letters to *The Kate Smith Hour*. Collins agreed to raise Bud and Lou's salary to $500 a week, and Sam Weisbord insisted on a year's contract. Bud and Lou remained with the show for ninety-nine weeks, rising to $1,250 a performance. At every broadcast Bud's sister Babe sat in the front row of the studio audience. She had a warm throaty laugh that Lou loved, and it inevitably induced the rest of the audience to laughter, even on the most inane of lines. So long and hearty were the laughs that Collins had trouble timing the show. A routine that measured six minutes at rehearsal stretched to ten at the broadcast. Collins established a timing system with Bud: "Whenever I poke you in the ribs, cut from wherever you are to the last line."

"Who's on First?" had proved so popular that Collins ordered it repeated every month. Even so, Bud and Lou started running low on material. They had been drawing on their supply of burlesque routines, and Bud realized that they were reaching the bottom of the barrel. Lou disagreed.

"Whadya mean, run out of funny stuff?" Lou challenged. "With repeats we can use our old burlesque gags for five years."

"Yeah, and the audience will get bored with us," Bud replied. "They'll go for 'Who's on First?' over and over again, but otherwise they want fresh material. There isn't that much stuff we can do on radio. How're we going to do the Lemon Table? Or 'Slowly I Turned'? Or Floogle Street? You gotta see that stuff."

"I think Bud's right," said Eddie Sherman. "I think you need a scriptwriter."

"What do I need a script for?" Lou replied. "I never had a script in burlesque, and they laughed, didn't they?"

"Yes, Lou, but you had a different audience every performance, and you moved from city to city," Sherman said. "In radio you got the same audience week after week, and you're competing against all the big shows. You gotta give 'em something new."

"I know a guy who'd be great for us," Bud said. "John Grant. I worked with him once in Detroit. That guy knew more comedy routines than anybody in the business."

"Yeah, I heard of John Grant," Lou said. "So what?"

"So I suggest we hire him," Bud replied.

"Not with my money you don't," Lou said flatly. "I'm not gonna spend dough on material we don't need."

"Boys, I got a solution," said Sherman. "We'll get Collins to pay for John Grant. That's only right, since you're going to do the routines on the Kate Smith show. Then you'll be able to keep the routines for other uses."

"Sounds good!" Bud agreed.

"Okay," said Lou, "but he don't get a dime out of my pocket."

He appeared at the door of the dressing room one day at CBS, wearing a heavy topcoat and a gray fedora with the brim turned up. With his steel-rimmed glasses he had the air of a prosperous undertaker. "I'm John Grant," he announced. He had brought with him two typewritten copies of a comedy routine. Lou was at first antagonistic. Bud persuaded him to run through the dialogue. Midway through their delivery Lou started laughing. When he reached the last page, he was laughing so hard he could hardly recite the lines.

"Hey, that's funny," Lou exclaimed.

"Terrific material," Bud agreed.

"You got any more like it?" Lou asked.

"As much as you need," said Grant, who had watched the impromptu performance without smiling.

John Grant was forty-seven, although he looked older. He

The Steel Pier marquee in later years, with the boys as top-dollar
headliners (they drew $150 a week when they started
in a minstrel show).

The gentle genius Eddie Sherman—as usual, in the middle

was born in Tarentum, Pennsylvania, and had left home to enter show business at an early age. He acted in operettas and appeared in vaudeville acts, but he concluded that he had no real future as a performer. His talents lay elsewhere, as he discovered when he went into burlesque. His knowledge of comedy was encyclopedic, and he could stage a new show every week for a year without repeating material. Circuit owners hired him to travel from one theater to another, rearranging casts, restaging production numbers and injecting new comedy that brought vast improvement to the performance. Grant realized the burlesque era was fading and he was looking for a new field of endeavor when the opportunity arose with Abbott and Costello. It was a happy confluence for both sides. John Grant was assured of steady income, and Bud and Lou were guaranteed a limitless supply of comedy material.

7

The Besting of Bobby Clark

BOBBY CLARK strode through the stage door of the Broadhurst Theater with his brisk, businesslike gait. Without the painted-on glasses, outrageous hats, and noisy plaids he affected onstage, he resembled an aging shoe salesman. He was plain-looking and small—he seemed even smaller in the camel's-hair topcoat he sported despite the warm May afternoon.

"Hello, Mr. Clark," the doorman said, and the comedian answered with a wave of his cigar.

He made his way through the cluster of performers backstage. They stared at him admiringly. They would be his supporting players in *The Streets of Paris*, the new revue being produced by the Shubert Brothers with Olsen and Johnson. His manner left no doubt that Bobby Clark was the star. Most of the other cast members were virtually unknown to the public; Clark had been acclaimed for two decades. He and his partner Paul McCullough had risen from burlesque to vaudeville, then starred in Broadway musicals and movie shorts. After McCullough's death, Clark achieved even greater prominence as a solo performer. He was the master of comic "business"; no one could milk a prop, a zany walk, a sleight of hand for more laughter than could Bobby Clark.

"Good afternoon, Bobby," said a voice as Clark walked confidently onto the empty stage. He peered over the footlights and saw the familiar face of Edward Duryea Dowling, who was directing *The Streets of Paris.*

"Hello, Eddie," Clark said with a scowl. "When do we start?"

"Today, Bobby, I thought we would begin by having the cast do their stuff," said Dowling. "A good way to get acquainted, don't you think?"

"You mean do something cold? I can't do that."

"No, not you, Bobby. I mean the other artists. Come on down here and watch with me."

Dowling and Clark sat in the front row as each member of the cast in turn handed music to the pianist and performed their most surefire routines. Dr. Think-a-Drink Hoffman waved his hands and produced martinis and whiskey sours from nowhere. Jean Sablon sang moody, romantic French songs. Luella Gear did a comic monologue, and Ben Dova lurched through his drunk routine. Carmen Miranda brought along a group of Brazilian percussionists to assist with her tongue-tripping Portuguese songs.

"They're all great, don't you think, Bobby?" asked Dowling.

"Tip-top," the comedian agreed. "What about those two comics? Where are they?"

"Abbott and Costello? They sent word they'd be late. They're doing four shows at the Roxy, as well as the Casa Mañana for Billy Rose every night."

"Maybe they're too busy," Clark said edgily.

The stage manager announced that Abbott and Costello had arrived, and soon the pair came onstage. They displayed none of the tentativeness of the other performers. Lou paused to talk to a couple of chorus girls while Bud walked to the stage apron and asked Dowling, "What d'ya want? The Lemon Table Bit? The Mustard Routine? The Hole in the Wall?"

"How about Mustard?" Dowling suggested.

"Ya got it!" Bud replied. "Now where the hell's my partner?"

While Bud went to separate Lou from the chorus girls, Bobby Clark muttered to Dowling, "The Mustard Routine! McCullough and I did that in burlesque thirty years ago."

The legendary Bobby Clark meets his match

The other performers took seats in the theater and watched expectantly as Bud and Lou approached each other from opposite sides of the stage. Bud grabbed Lou by the arm and demanded, "Hey, Lou, where you going in such a hurry?"

"I'm gonna get myself something to eat, Abbott," Lou replied. "Boy, am I hungry!"

"What are you going to get?"

"I wanna great big hot dog—without mustard."

Bud reacted as if he had been insulted. Why didn't Lou want mustard? Lou replied innocently that he disliked mustard on his hot dogs. Mustard made him sick. If he was sick, he couldn't work. If he couldn't work, he couldn't support his wife and children. His children would end up in an orphan asylum. Is that what Bud wanted? Lou painted such a mournful picture of the consequences that the audience was convulsed.

"What are you, some kind of big shot, that you won't eat mustard?" Bud demanded. Lou remained defiant, but now Bud began his assault. He outlined the process of manufacturing

69

mustard, how thousands of people were employed in the process. What would happen if others like Lou stopped eating mustard? All of those people would be walking the streets looking for jobs. Bud depicted the economic and personal disaster that would result from the rejection of mustard. Lou tried to resist the onslaught, but Bud was relentless. Finally Lou admitted his wrong-headedness in an outburst of anguish, and the professional audience exploded in laughter and applause.

Even Bobby Clark had to admit that it had been a masterpiece of comedy timing and invention. "These boys will bear watching," he said.

Clark himself was a master of invention, and he reached deep into his time-worn bag for pieces of business and costuming. He and the two new émigrés from burlesque competed in their own sketches and then met head-on in "That's Music," a zany charade in a Paris music shop. During an out-of-town performance, Clark happened to drop his beret. Lou grabbed a hat rack, Bud produced a cane, and together they played the beret

With the man who wrote the stuff, John Grant

like a hockey puck. Clark was temporarily awed. But at the next performance Bud scored the beret under a phonograph, and Clark blasted a referee's whistle to signal the goal.

Opening night at the Broadhurst was June 19, 1939. Eddie Sherman realized that the premiere performance was crucial to the careers of his clients. If Abbott and Costello could score with the critics and the audience amid the cast of Bobby Clark, Carmen Miranda, Jean Sablon, and other superior performers, they would emerge as stars. Success on radio was ephemeral. Making big salaries in movie theaters and New York night clubs impressed the trade. But only a Broadway show—or a hit movie—carried the prestige of real stardom.

Sherman had his own case of opening-night jitters as he made his way through the backstage crowd of musicians and performers. He knocked on the dressing room marked "Abbott and Costello," and Lou's voice called, "Come on in." Sherman was astonished to find Bud and Lou sitting in their underwear facing each other over a deck of cards.

"Oh, hi, Eddie. You wanna get in the game?" Lou said, drawing a card from the stack.

"Lou, Bud, I'm astonished!" Sherman exclaimed.

"Whassamatter, you never seen us in shorts before?" said Bud, laying down a card.

"Don't you boys realize that the curtain goes up in twenty minutes?" Sherman said. "You're not even dressed yet."

"We got time," Lou said, continuing the game.

"But shouldn't you be going over your cues?" said Sherman. "This is Broadway, you know, not burlesque."

Lou gazed up from his study of the cards. "Are there people out there?" he asked.

"Of course," said Sherman. "The theater is packed."

"Are they breathing?" Lou asked.

"Of course," Sherman said.

"If they're out there an' they're breathing, that's all I need to know. We'll kill 'em."

It happened as Lou predicted. Each Abbott and Costello sketch brought cascades of laughter that had rarely been heard in a Broadway theater, not even in the *Hellzapoppin'* of coproducers Olsen and Johnson. The peak came in "Rest Cure," which was nothing more than the tried-and-true Crazy House Routine reworked with variations by John Grant. It began with Lou arriving at a sanitarium for a rest, not realizing that he had entered an insane asylum. He grew suspicious when the buxom blond nurse showed him to a room, insisting on absolute quiet, then screaming, *"Mr. Lou Costello is here!"*

His suspicions were confirmed when the doctor arrived. He was Bud Abbott, in fright wig and smock dabbed with red paint, peering at Lou through thick glasses and saying, "Come here, little girl, I'm not going to hurt you." All the patient needed was a good rest, said the doctor, exiting with a maniacal laugh. Lou peeled down to a nightshirt and was tucked in bed by the cooing nurse.

A mad parade of visitors forestalled Lou's sleep. A man pounded playing cards with a hammer; his explanation: "I'm playing knock rummy." A swami asked if Lou wanted his palm read; Lou agreed, and his hand was daubed with red paint. A loony set down a valise and stepped over it; "I just got over the grippe," he explained. A woman mistook Lou's bed for a flower garden and sprinkled it from a watering can.

"He's a pump! Pump him!" said a frantic woman of her companion, who extended one arm. Lou pumped and won a squirt of water in the face. Lou was subjected to gun battles and a firing squad that drowned him with seltzer bottles. Drenched and exhausted, he collapsed into bed, then watched as an airy female plucked imaginary apples from an invisible tree. She left as Lou pondered his own sanity. He walked to the "tree," shook it—and was knocked out by a shower of real apples.

When the time came for curtain calls, the cheers were loudest for Abbott and Costello. Bud was beaming, Lou remained nonchalant. Carmen Miranda stood beside him in her Brazilian costume, including headdress of artificial fruit. Unknown to her, Lou had planted a real banana there. As the curtain call continued, he removed and peeled the banana and stuffed it into his mouth.

Brooks Atkinson wrote in his *Times* review: "Abbott is the

overbearing mastermind whose feverish, impatient guidance of the conversation produces the crisis. Costello is the short, fat he-who-gets-slapped. He is a moon-faced zany with wide, credulous eyes, a high voice, and puffy hands that struggle in futile gestures. Both men work themselves into a state of excitement that is wonderful to behold."

The Broadhurst audiences agreed. They had rarely seen such vitality, such disdain for theatrical artifice. No stage actor would consider stopping a sketch in midpassage to address the audience. Lou did. When a woman patron arose and started to leave the theater on a mission of obvious urgency, he stepped to the footlights and bawled, "Hey, lady, don't leave; we ain't finished yet." The flustered woman started to return, then Lou cracked, "If you gotta go, you gotta go. The ladies' room is downstairs and to the right." If a patron arrived late, Lou stepped out of character and explained what had happened in the show thus far. The audience roared.

Lou never gave the same performance twice. He was so inventive and unpredictable that other members of *The Streets of Paris* cast stood in the wings to watch him. Even Bobby Clark.

The Streets of Paris shared a Broadway season that included Katharine Hepburn in *The Philadelphia Story*, Fredric March and Florence Eldridge in *The American Way*, Howard Lindsay and Dorothy Stickney in *Life with Father*, Monty Woolley in *The Man Who Came to Dinner*, Paul Muni in *Key Largo*, Raymond Massey in *Abe Lincoln of Illinois*, Gertrude Lawrence in *Skylark*, Vivien Leigh and Laurence Olivier in *Romeo and Juliet*. Lou Costello was unimpressed at being amid such distinguished company. To him the legitimate theater was no different from burlesque. His goal remained elsewhere.

"That face!" he muttered as he gazed into his dressing-room mirror. "I gotta get that face in movies."

Not yet. Eddie Sherman and the William Morris office were husbanding the Abbott and Costello career with care and foresight. When *The Streets of Paris* closed in February 1940, Bud and Lou were booked into movie houses at salaries of $3,500 a week. They became favorites at the cavernous Roxy in New

York and played there three times in a year. Bud and Lou had helped *The Kate Smith Hour* to overtake Rudy Vallee in the audience ratings, and Abbott and Costello became stars of their own summer radio show, replacing Fred Allen. Mike Todd bought the rights to *The Streets of Paris* and restaged the show at the New York World's Fair starring Abbott and Costello and Gypsy Rose Lee.

Bud and Lou were appearing on radio every week, playing four shows at the Fair, then hurrying to the Versailles night club to perform at the midnight show. The routine seemed undemanding after the rigors of the burlesque life, but the strains were beginning to show. During most of their four years together, they had been too occupied with survival to analyze their relationship. Their attitude toward each other was one of mutual need and protection. Now success was theirs, and the stresses were materializing, like tiny cracks in a Chinese glaze. A sharp word here, a deprecating remark there. Racing from radio studio to theater to night club, living distantly in Long Island and Paterson, each hearing his wife and relatives say how great *he* was and how little his partner contributed. It was easy for the onstage bickering to transfer to the dressing room. To the bystander their offstage arguments sounded comical, like variations on the theme of "Who's on First?" But their exchanges bore the sharp edge of reality. And their gambling grew more intense. Lou, like Bud, had learned to gamble as relief from the backstage boredom of burlesque and the tedium of continual travel. They played rummy and poker together, and as their salaries climbed, so did the stakes. So did each one's enjoyment of beating his partner.

Lou delighted in berating Bud after a win at cards.

"Yeah," Bud replied, "don't forget who's name comes first. It's Abbott and Costello, not Costello and Abbott."

"That's all right," Lou replied. "Some day you'll end up working for me."

8

Hollywood

MOVIE COMEDY had fallen to a low estate by 1940. Charlie Chaplin produced *The Great Dictator,* but it was his first film in four years. Harold Lloyd had retired to his estate, and Buster Keaton was doing bit parts. Paramount had dropped W. C. Fields, and M-G-M was about to do the same with the Marx Brothers. Laurel and Hardy moved from M-G-M to 20th Century-Fox for another string of cheap comedies, and Bob Hope, the vaudevillian and radio comedian, was struggling to escape from the Paramount B factory.

With comedy no longer king, Hollywood was slow to respond to the burgeoning success of Abbott and Costello. Talent reports flowed from New York offices to the California studios, and the comments were unpromising: "They're radio comics—too verbal for motion pictures"; "They're burlesque comics—too blue for movies."

Yet studio executives were aware that Bud and Lou had scored in *The Streets of Paris,* that they drew big grosses when they appeared in stage shows of Eastern movie houses. Children everywhere were repeating "I'm a ba-a-a-ad boy!" and reciting the litany of "Who's on First?" Palpably, Abbott and Costello could no longer be ignored.

Metro-Goldwyn-Mayer made the first offer. The studio was beefing up its musicals, assembling a number of specialty

The first movie, One Night in the Tropics—*with Allan Jones (left) and Bob Cummings*

acts to add entertainment value. M-G-M was willing to pay Abbott and Costello $17,500 per film to perform one or two of their routines. "I don't like it," Eddie Sherman said. "Bud and Lou should have their own pictures, not just guest shots in somebody else's."

Matty Fox, a New York executive of Universal Pictures, called Sherman to inquire if the M-G-M contract had been signed. When Sherman said no, Fox suggested a conference. He proposed that Bud and Lou appear in a Universal musical, doing their routines for $35,000. Even though Bud and Lou would not be starring, it seemed like a good place to start in films, and the salary was double what M-G-M had offered. Bud and Lou would have a better chance of being noticed at Universal than at M-G-M, which boasted of more stars than there are in the heavens. And so they went West, Bud for the first time, Lou in pursuit of the success that had eluded him a dozen years before. They would be billed after Allan Jones, Robert Cummings, Nancy Kelly and Mary Boland in a film called *One Night in the Tropics*. The story had originated in an Earl Derr Biggers novel that Universal owned, *Love Insurance*, but had undergone enough script rewrites to render its origin unrecognizable. Jerome Kern had written some songs, with lyrics by Oscar Hammerstein II and Dorothy Fields; none was memorable except a ballad, "Remind Me," which was played with a rhumba beat over Kern's heated objections. A young screen writer, Leonard Spigelgass, was assigned by the studio to produce the film.

"We've got the plot, all those songs, and Abbott and Costello," Spigelgass protested to a Universal executive. "How can we handle all three elements in one picture?"

"Fuck the plot," he was told.

Such was the unpromising project that awaited Bud and Lou in Universal City. At that point in its history, Universal Pictures was undergoing one of its periodic bad times. Founder-king Carl Laemmle had been deposed in 1936, along with his crown prince, Junior Laemmle. A money man named J. Cheever Cowdin, whose experience had been largely with aircraft companies, assumed control of the teetering company as chairman of the board; president was Nate J. Blumberg, a veteran of the theater circuits. Studio operations were conducted by a committee, always in Hollywood studios a sure sign of disarray. The committee members were longtime theater men; vice president and general manager was Cliff Work, a former exhibitor from San Francisco. During conferences in his studio office, he sometimes disappeared under his desk, confounding those who didn't know that he was a tobacco chewer with a periodic need of a cuspidor. Since the palace coup against the Laemmles, the major asset of Universal had been the sunny young soprano, Deanna Durbin. But she had matured, and her films were not as popular as they had been during her pubescence. This caused shudders of concern among the onetime ticket takers who ran Universal Studio.

The director of *One Night in the Tropics* was A. Edward Sutherland, a London-born graduate of the Keystone Cops. He was unfamiliar with the world of burlesque, and Bud and Lou were unacquainted with the methods of filming. During their years in burlesque, radio and theater, they had always recited their routines from the beginning. So when Sutherland yelled

"Cut!" in the middle of their recital, they were unable to continue. They had to return to the beginning and start all over again.

The efforts of four screen writers were not enough to elevate *One Night in the Tropics* from the humdrum to the mediocre. Midway through the filming it became evident that Abbott and Costello provided the only note of originality. Instead of merely having them perform their routines, they were integrated into the plot as operatives of the villainous William Frawley.

Bud and Lou finished their brief duty in Universal City and returned to New York. When *One Night in the Tropics* was previewed in Huntington Park, an industrial suburb favored by the studios because of its average-citizen audience, the movie was greeted with expectable apathy—except when Bud and Lou came on the screen. Their very appearance delighted the audience, and much of their rapid diaolgue was obscured by laughter. Even the slow-witted production committee could perceive the message, and it was transmitted to Matty Fox in New York. He summoned Bud and Lou and Eddie Sherman to a meeting in his office.

"That was a nice job you boys did for us," said Fox, a shrewd negotiator. "What are you going to do next?"

"Oh, we got a deal coming up at Paramount," said Lou, astonishing Bud and Eddie Sherman.

"Paramount, huh?" said Fox. "What kind of pictures did you have in mind to do?"

"Well, I think we oughta make an army picture," Lou said. "Lotsa guys getting drafted nowadays, and Bud and I got some routines that'll fit right in. We could do the Drill Scene. Let's show him the Drill Scene, Bud." They did the Drill Scene, and Fox was convulsed. "Then we could do the Dice Game. Let's do the Dice Game, Bud." They performed the routine with the same result, as well as the Packing and Unpacking.

"That's great, fellas," Fox said. "You got any ideas for other pictures?"

"Yeah, we oughta do a ghost picture," Lou said. "Let's show him the 'Oh, Charlie,' Bud."

After they finished, Fox wiped the tears from his eyes and said, "Don't go to Paramount. Stick with Universal. We'll give you a seven-year contract and you'll star in your own pictures."

"Not a bad idea," Lou said, grinning broadly.

The four men met again in California to negotiate a contract, and they were joined by Abe Lastfogel, as agent for Bud and Lou, and Cliff Work and studio manager Edward Muhl, representing the company. Universal offered a deal for four films a year at $50,000 per film. Lastfogel and Sherman wanted $60,000. Neither side could concede, and Sherman made another proposal: Bud and Lou would accept $50,000 per picture plus ten percent of the profits. The Universal negotiators were astonished. No actor in films received a percentage of the profits. Instinctively the company men rejected the proposal. Sherman fought for it.

Lou summoned Sherman into the hall and said: "What the hell are you doing, Eddie? You'll queer the deal with this percentage-of-the-profits business."

"I don't think so, Lou," said Sherman. "I think they'd rather give you a cut of future profits than shell out the forty grand a year. If your pictures make profits, then everybody wins."

"Yeah, but I'd rather have the forty grand myself."

"Lou, I'll make you a deal. If any picture doesn't bring you at least ten thousand in profits, I won't charge you any commission."

Lou's serious face brightened. "In that case, go ahead."

Predictably, the Universal executives were more concerned about saving $40,000 ($10,000 apiece for four films) a year than giving away a percentage of nebulous profits. After all, *One Night in the Tropics* had done only fair business despite the presence of Abbott and Costello, and there was no assurance that their starring films would perform any better. Universal agreed to the ten-percent clause and thereby divested itself of $1 million on the first four Abbott and Costello films.

9

Buck Privates, Stardom, and an Ominous Aftermath

"I'VE ONLY GOT one ambition in my life, and I've had it since I was a boy. I want to be a movie star. I came out here when I was a kid and I tried it. I nearly got myself killed as a stunt man and I nearly died of starvation. I went back East with my tail between my legs. Now I got another chance and I gotta make it. I gotta! I've been a star in burlesque, in radio, and on Broadway. They don't mean a thing. I want to be a movie star. If you can help me do that, I'll never give you a moment's trouble, I swear on my mother's honor I won't."

An honest expression, though a poor prediction. Lou was pouring out his aspirations to Alex Gottlieb, the man who was going to produce Bud and Lou's first starring film, *Buck Privates.* Gottlieb was impressed. He had faith that Lou's hope would be achieved, though few others at Universal Studio did.

Russian-born, a graduate of the University of Wisconsin, Gottlieb had been a reporter on the Brooklyn *Eagle,* drifted into movie publicity, and finally screen writing. He had finished writing a comedy for Hugh Herbert when the Universal executive producer, Milton Feld, asked him, "How would you like to be a producer?"

"I think I would," replied the ambitious Gottlieb.

"The studio has signed a couple of comics for a series of B pictures," Feld explained.

"You mean Abbott and Costello?"

"Yes. Have you ever seen them?"

"Sure, I saw them in *The Streets of Paris* in New York."

"What do you think of them?"

"You can make B pictures with them if you want, but I'll make you a prediction: Within one year they'll be the Number One stars at the box office," Gottlieb said.

Feld smiled patronizingly. "Now, Alex. They're just a couple of low comics."

"Maybe so, but I'll tell you something. When I saw them in New York, I looked around the audience. There were stockbrokers and salesgirls, and they all were laughing! All of them. I never saw anyone who could make an entire audience laugh. They strike the lowest common denominator of comedy."

"Perhaps they do, but don't start getting any ideas about making A pictures with them. The studio doesn't have that in mind."

"Could I ask you something?" Gottlieb put in.

"What's that?" Feld said.

"Why me?"

"Well," Feld explained, "we wanted a comedy writer to produce their pictures, so he would understand how to put the script together. Why you? Because we were turned down by twenty other writers who said Abbott and Costello were just burlesque comics."

Gottlieb began work on the script of *Buck Privates* with the writer of the original screenplay, Arthur T. Horman. Together they developed the formula which would continue through the movie career of Bud and Lou. The script would consist of four or five Abbott and Costello routines surrounded but not confined by a plot. The routines were supplied by John Grant, who at first received screen credit for special material but in subsequent films was listed as co-writer.

As the script was being prepared, Bud brought Betty to California, and Lou came with Anne and their two daughters. Since they were starring in the film, both Bud and Lou were required to undergo physical examinations for the customary insurance against loss of production time due to illness. Bud passed, despite his epilepsy. Lou didn't.

"What's the matter?" Lou asked.

"I don't like your heart action, Mr. Costello," said the studio doctor.

"Whadya mean? I've never been sick in my life."

"I'm sorry. I can't pass you."

Lou was panicked. "I can't blow it now. Tell me what I can do so I can pass the test."

"For one thing," said the doctor, gazing at the cigar Lou had smoked throughout the examination, "you could stop smoking for a while. Then in another month or two we'll examine you again and see if that has helped." In what he felt to be a great sacrifice—Lou loved his cigars—Lou gave up smoking for two months, then passed the physical examination. He resumed the cigars but lighted them less often. The doctor's report had disquieted him.

Arthur Lubin was assigned to direct *Buck Privates*. When he was told that he would be working with Abbott and Costello he replied, "I think you'd better get a dance director." He had confused Bud and Lou with the Muriel Abbott Dancers, a popular dance group. Lubin was a meticulous man, schooled in the theater as an actor and director—a curious choice to guide the first starring film of two earthy comedians. Bud gave a party to initiate the filmmaking family, and Lubin seemed to have little in common with his two stars or their burlesque-educated wives. But he was impressed by the will of Bud and Lou to succeed, especially Lou. Both would arrive an hour and a half early for a nine o'clock call. The director was impressed with Lou's instinct for precision timing, his uncanny knack of knowing how long to maintain a take and when to win the audience with a smile. Lubin also appreciated Bud's discipline, returning Lou to the main path after he tried to diverge from the script. Lubin provided the benefit of his own talent, hitting Bud and Lou with light when they were in focus and providing an artistic balance when they were offscreen.

Let us consider the alchemy of *Buck Privates* and why it

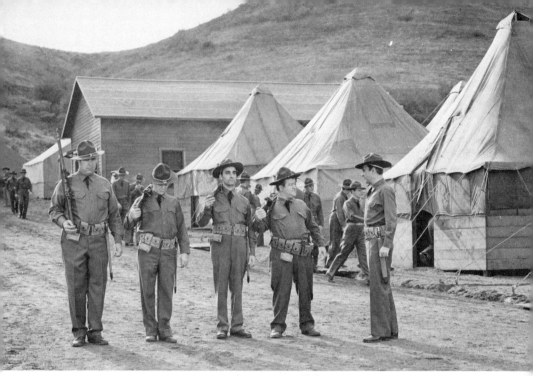

From Buck Privates: *the famous drill routine . . . and the fight scene—with Nat Pendleton as referee*

made stars of Bud and Lou. It bears the gloss of the Hollywood product of the late thirties and early forties; although Universal's films were largely made by second-class talents, its films were technically the equal of the bigger studios, excepting M-G-M. Universal's aspirations were never high; it sought only to provide adequate entertainment, usually for the lower half of the double bill. *Buck Privates* succeeded not only because it was entertaining, but topical as well. It began with President Roosevelt signing the draft law in a Universal Newsreel clip. The script offered a host of draft jokes and situations, some dating back to World War I and perhaps the Civil War. The cast included the Andrews Sisters, who sang three hit songs, "Apple Blossom Time," "The Boogie-Woogie Bugle Boy of Company B," and "You're a Lucky Fellow, Mr. Smith."

Bud and Lou were introduced in typical guise, as pitchman and shill hawking ties on a downtown sidewalk. Chanted Bud: "I've lived on the bounty of the county, and I done my boardin' with the warden. Never have I ever had the opportunity of presenting such merchandise. Feel the material—that's enough." Nat Pendleton, ever the big dumb cop, came along to break up the pitch, and Bud and Lou escaped into what they thought was a theater; it was actually a draft center. They are inducted, along with a snobby playboy, Lee Bowman, and his nice-guy chauffeur, Alan Curtis. Both vied for the affections of army hostess June Frazee; romance was obligatory in the early Abbott and Costello films, as it was in the comedies of the Marx Brothers, Martin and Lewis, etc. The romance alternated with the Andrews Sisters songs and the A&C routines, lifted almost unchanged from burlesque.

The executives of Universal were beginning to sense the box-office potential of Abbott and Costello. Four weeks after finishing *Buck Privates*, Bud and Lou started work on *Hold That Ghost*, which employed the haunted-house routines they had auditioned in Matty Fox's office. Alex Gottlieb produced, Arthur Lubin directed, and John Grant's contributions earned him credit as coauthor of the screen play. It was a tale of ghosts and gangsters, with the Andrews Sisters again providing musical numbers, and Richard Carlson and Evelyn Ankers playing the young lovers.

Buck Privates was released on February 3, 1941, with astonishing results. The $180,000 movie with a couple of burlesque comics, lately on radio, was outdrawing such prestigious films as *How Green Was My Valley, Citizen Kane, Here Comes Mr. Jordan, Sergeant York,* and *Blossoms in the Dust.* Even the New York critics, ordinarily unimpressed by low comedy, were admiring. The *Times:* "Army humor isn't apt to be subtle and neither are Abbott and Costello. Their antics have as much innuendo as a thousand-pound bomb, but nearly as much explosive force." The *Herald-Tribune:* "It's hard to imagine how any future films in the series can be any funnier than *Buck Privates,* for Abbott and Costello have few equals in their particular field of comedy and they take to army life as cows take to pasture."

Alas for Universal, it had sold *Buck Privates* as it would any other B picture—at bargain prices. So the millions of dollars in profits provided by delighted moviegoers went largely to theaters and theater chains. It was a mistake that Universal was certain not to repeat. Within one year the company would release four more films starring Bud and Lou, at terms more equitable.

No sooner had Alex Gottlieb finished producing *Hold That Ghost* than Universal decided it would be prudent to follow *Buck Privates* with a picture about the navy. Arthur Horman conceived a story and John Grant embellished it with routines. Gottlieb marveled at Grant's facility. On one occasion Grant produced a complete routine overnight. It seemed faintly familiar to Gottlieb, and he showed it to Bud. "Never heard it before," said Bud. Gottlieb decided to consult a book he owned, *A Compendium of Humor for All Occasions,* written in 1870. Grant's routine was there.

Despite the success of *Buck Privates,* Universal still affixed a B-picture budget to *In the Navy,* and Gottlieb had to seek ways to give the film more quality. For the romantic lead, he found a good name at a bargain price. Dick Powell had been dropped by Warner Brothers after his vogue as a musical star had dwindled. "I'm a forgotten man; nobody wants to hire me," he lamented to Gottlieb. Would he appear in a picture with Abbott and Costello? "Yes, I'll do it," Powell said, adding, "Even though I'm a forgotten man, I've been a star. I'll do it only if I get star billing." And so it was "Abbott and Costello and Dick Powell *In the Navy*."

During the preparedness period of 1941, the armed services were eager for publicity, and Gottlieb saved production money by acquiring permission to photograph navy ships and bases. The admirals were outraged when the final film was submitted for approval. The final sequence, filmed with miniatures at Salton Sea and real ships at Pearl Harbor, was a chase with Lou as a disguised admiral giving orders for hilarious maneuvers. "An insult!" cried the admirals, refusing to allow release of the film with the offending sequence. Universal executives were in a panic. The chase ran a reel in length and was the highlight of *In the Navy*. Gottlieb asked permission for a morning's retakes. He filmed a scene in which Bud struck Lou on the head with a frying pan during an argument. Unconscious, Lou dreamed the entire chase. On that basis, the Navy Department gave its approval of the movie.

And so *Buck Privates* begat *Hold That Ghost*, which begat *In the Navy*, which begat *Keep 'Em Flying*, which begat *Ride 'Em Cowboy*, all within a 12-month span. Never did a string of B pictures earn so much. This astounded the more sophisticated critics, who could not fathom the Abbott and Costello appeal. Their comedy was so elemental as to defy analysis; James Agee dismissed Bud and Lou as "semi-skilled laborers, at best." Neither possessed an ounce of sex appeal. Bud was forty-six years old, with plain features and a raspy voice, and his badgering of his defenseless partner made him unsympathetic. Lou as the fall guy evoked sympathy, but he was scarcely a romantic figure, with his rotundity and cigars. Despite the absence of the customary movie-star appeal, Bud and Lou found themselves by late 1941 voted the No. 3 moneymaking stars by the theater owners of America, following Mickey Rooney and Clark Gable.

Bud and Lou had been introduced to a new and glorious

86

In the Navy *had Dick Powell . . . and the
Andrews Sisters—Laverne, Patty, and Maxene*

Deanna Durbin (below) *was the big star
at Universal—but not for long*

world, and they reveled in it. To both of them, family meant everything, and they gathered their relatives around them. Bud bought a house for his sister Olive and her two children, Norman and Betty, and Babe Abbott came to California, too. Lou persuaded his mother and father to leave Paterson for the gentler climate of the San Fernando Valley. Pat Costello became Lou's stand-in and double. Lou's sister, Marie, and her husband, Joe Kirk, came West as well, and Joe acted in most of the A&C movies.

As we have noted, Lou promised not to give the studio a moment's trouble if he achieved his ambition of becoming a movie star. He kept that promise until the third picture.

The queen of Universal remained Deanna Durbin, whose musicals had been the studio's best-selling product until the advent of Bud and Lou. The studio had provided her with a large house trailer which could be moved from stage to stage and to locations. No other star was accorded such a courtesy. On a Saturday afternoon Lou visited the office of Morris Davis, a Universal executive.

"Bud and I want trailers like Durbin has, one for him, one for me," Lou announced. Davis argued on the studio's behalf, declaring that the trailers would be an extraordinary expense, would occupy too much space on stages, etc.

"I want those trailers, Morrie," Lou responded.

"Lou, I just explained to you why the studio can't provide them," Davis said.

"Okay, Morrie, if you say so," said Lou.

"I'm glad you're being reasonable about this, Lou."

"Of course I'm reasonable. I'm always reasonable. And I want you to know what I'm gonna report to work on time Monday. I'm gonna know all my lines and I'll do everything the director asks me to do." He took a puff on his cigar, walked to the door and turned. "But I don't know how funny I'll be."

Identical trailers appeared on the set the following Monday, and they remained fixtures on all Abbott and Costello films.

Lou had changed in another, more serious way: his attitude toward Bud.

The easy backstage camaraderie of New York had vanished. Bud always referred to Lou as "my little partner," but Bud was always "Abbott" to Lou. Fame had been bestowed on them equally, but Lou did not consider theirs an equal partnership. Finally his feelings came into the open. He summoned Eddie Sherman to his home.

"I got news for you, little man," said Lou who always used the cognomen although he and Sherman were almost the same height.

"What is it, Lou?" asked Eddie, vaguely apprehensive about Lou's serious attitude.

"You remember the time we got that offer to play Atlantic City when we were in burlesque?"

"Of course I do. That was our first big break."

"And you remember that Bud didn't want to take the deal, he wanted to stay in burlesque?"

"Yes, I remember, Lou."

"And you remember that, in order to convince him, I agreed to give him ten bucks out of my cut?"

"Yes."

"Okay. Now you go tell Bud that from now on we split our movie dough sixty–forty or I don't work with him."

Eddie was stunned. Lou had never given the slightest hint that he would make such a demand. "Lou, you can't be serious," he said.

"You think I would kid about something like this?"

"No, I guess you wouldn't. But I wish you would think about it."

"I *have* been thinking about it," Lou said excitedly. "I've been thinking about it for five years now, ever since Bud pulled that on me. Well, he's going to pay for it now."

"Lou, I gotta tell you I think you're completely off base. The money doesn't mean that much to you. You're gonna be making more money than you'll know what to do with. Think what this would do to Bud. He's got his pride, you know."

"Yeah? Well, he shoulda thought about mine five years ago."

"This could hurt the team very deeply. You *need* Bud, Lou."

"Bullshit. I could paint him on a backdrop, that's how much I need him."

"I wish you would change your mind."

"No chance. Now go to Bud and give him the news. And there's something else."

"What's that?"

"We're changing the billing. From now on it's Costello and Abbott."

"Change the billing!"

"Costello and Abbott. That's the way it's going to be."

"But that's impossible. Everybody knows you as Abbott and Costello."

"Not anymore. Now go deliver your message."

"Lou——"

"That's it, little man."

Eddie Sherman didn't deliver the message to Bud. He returned to Lou's house the following day and tried to dissuade him from the ruinous course. Lou was more adamant than before. More days of argument. Finally Lou said, "Starting with the next picture, it's a sixty-forty split or I won't work with Bud anymore. Go tell him. Now."

With heavy heart, Eddie Sherman made an appointment to see Bud at his house one evening, advising him to invite his attorney, Nate Friedman. Eddie outlined Lou's decision. Bud's first reaction was anger.

"That ungrateful bastard," Bud said. "He'd still be doing pratfalls in burlesque if it wasn't for me. He'd be nothing without me."

Bud continued in that vein, and Eddie let him. Then Eddie said, "Bud, I agree that Lou would be lost without you. He needs your strong hand to control him, your sternness to play off of. But you need him, too. I've argued and argued until I'm blue in the face. You know Lou as well as I do; once he gets a notion, there ain't nothin's going to change his mind."

"Supposing I just say no, I won't do it," Bud suggested.

"Then I'm afraid it means the breakup of the team," Eddie said sadly.

90

"You think Lou would do that?"

"I *know* he would. If I didn't think so, I wouldn't have come to you with his proposal."

"What do *you* think I should do?"

"I hate to say it, but I'm afraid you have to give Lou his sixty percent—unless you're willing to break up the team."

Bud's lawyer agreed. Bud sighed his assent. "My brother Harry was right," he said. "He told me, 'Beware of the Italian who gets rich.'"

Eddie Sherman then brought up Lou's other demand: that the billing be changed to Costello and Abbott.

"No!" Bud exploded. "Absolutely not! My name has always gone first, and that's the way it's going to stay. If he wants to break up the team over that, let him."

Eddie returned to Lou with Bud's decision. Lou was pleased that Bud had capitulated on the money split, but he raged over Bud's stubbornness on the billing. "It'll be Costello and Abbott whether he likes it or not," Lou declared. "You go tell Universal it's a new deal: a sixty–forty split and from now on it's Costello and Abbott."

Sherman argued no further, suspecting that events would solve the remaining difference. He was right. Universal executives did not care how the two stars divided their salaries but they would not entertain a change of billing. "We bought Abbott and Costello, not Costello and Abbott," they decreed.

Lou would not forget Bud's obduracy on the billing, nor could Bud forget being forced to shave his share of the take. When they returned to work at the studio, it was not the same as it had been before. The two-handed poker games in their trailers between takes became more feverish, and their insults seemed to have a biting edge. And when Bud assaulted Lou in a comedy routine, the slaps came harder.

10

A New Way of Life
for Bud and Lou

IN THOSE DAYS the movie studios maintained
propaganda ministries unmatched by any government in peace or
war. Star reporters and newspaper hacks by the hundreds trekked
to California and joined the legions in praise of the Hollywood
product. Publicity work was departmentalized. Each movie,
even the six-day quickies that Universal made, had a unit man to
record the day-to-day happenings. His writings were reviewed
by a copy-editor, who scrutinized the prose as severely as a *New
York Times* desk man. Feature writers, some trained to imitate
the style of certain columnists, also submitted stories. This tor-
rent of words was channeled to the planters, the conduits from
publicity mill to press. There was a planter for Louella and a
planter for Hedda, and they competed as fiercely as did the two
columnists. There was a city-side planter who hustled copy to
the local *Times, Examiner, Herald-Express, Daily News,* and
Hollywood Citizen-News. There were planters for the syndi-
cates, the trade papers, the national magazines, the fan magazines,
the out-of-town press, the foreign correspondents, the radio
shows. There were tie-up people, who arranged for stars to appear in cigarette ads ("Chesterfields are milder"—Bob Hope).
There were cheesecake photographers and glamour photographers and still men who set up their tripods after every scene
and said, "Hold it for a still."

All this machinery was turned on at Universal for the promotion of Bud and Lou when it appeared that they were going to assure the studio's solvency. Lou also brought out from New York his and Bud's own press agent, Joe Glaston, a round, slumped, earnest man with a hangdog expression earned through constant abuse from Bud and Lou. Glaston was especially adept at arranging meaningless but space-getting honors. Governor Julius ("the Just") Heil named Bud and Lou Wisconsin colonels. The Walnut Growers Association of California elected them "America's No. 1 Nuts." Governor Leverett Saltonstall asked them to make a film for the Massachusetts Department of Mental Health. Such achievements were not enough for Lou. "Get us more," he commanded Joe Glaston.

By the time of Bud and Lou's fourth starring film, *Keep 'Em Flying*, the Universal publicity department was willing to devote not only its creative energies but money as well. Publicity chief John Joseph asked his staff for ideas on how to exploit the film, and he budgeted $5,000 for the campaign. The department's photo editor, Kenneth Carter, a flying enthusiast, suggested the winning campaign. Why not, he proposed, have a gliding contest in three parts of the country, with Abbott and Costello as judges, the event to be covered by a coast-to-coast radio hookup? Joseph gave his approval, and Carter spent months in preparation for the December event. The glider association welcomed such recognition of its activities, and contests were scheduled in Los Angeles, Chicago, and Elmira, New York. CBS agreed to send radio crews to the three locations and broadcast the event nationally. It was scheduled for a Sunday so as not to interfere with Bud and Lou's shooting schedule and to assure a wide listenership and availability of the weekend glider pilots.

The morning of the big *Keep 'Em Flying* glider contest arrived. The western part was to take place at Vail Field, an airport for gliders east of Los Angeles. Carter had arranged everything, including the obligatory starlet, a contract player named Marie McDonald, who would arrive by air in a bathing suit. She and Carter took off from Van Nuys Airport in a small plane, and as they approached Vail Field, the press agent gazed down with satisfaction. Stretched along the runway was a line of thirty gliders, all painted in bright colors. Near the grandstand was the CBS remote truck, and there was a cluster of reporters and photographers, as well as tidy crowd of local citizens.

The plane landed, and Marie stepped out, expanded her chest and posed for a lineup of Speed Graphics. Two LaSalle limousines from the studio arrived, bringing Bud and Lou precisely on schedule. They posed with Marie, and Lou convulsed the photographers with comments about her attributes. Carter stood behind and beamed. He knew that, in Chicago and Elmira, Universal field representatives were at that moment preparing the start of the *Keep 'Em Flying* glider contest. With his concentration of the events before the cameras, he failed to notice a restless murmuring among the crowd, the reporters and photographers conversing with each other. Some of them started running to their cars. Then, to Carter's horror, he saw the CBS crew dismantle the microphones and head for the truck. He raced after them. "What's the matter? Where are you going?" he asked.

"We've been ordered to Long Beach to cover the takeoff of B-17s," said the crewman. "The Japs have bombed Pearl Harbor."

The war brought Bud and Lou even greater popularity. In three of their first four starring films, they were enlisted in the army, navy, and air corps. They were identified as the comic counterparts of millions of Americans who were entering the services; no one stopped to consider that Bud at forty-six was overage for a recruit. Their comedy was ideally suited for the time. It was topical and swift; Bud and Lou could deliver six jokes during one of Jack Benny's pauses. It was basic and noncerebral. And so, despite Universal's pennypinched budgets, Bud and Lou ascended in the first war year to No. 1 moneymaking stars in the poll of circuit and independent exhibitors of the United States, conducted by the *Motion Picture Herald*. Since the poll had originated ten years before, the position had been won twice by Marie Dressler, once by Will Rogers, four times by Shirley Temple, and twice by Mickey Rooney. None had risen as fast as Bud and Lou: They made it in less than two years.

Eddie Sherman did what agents are supposed to do: he announced to Universal that his clients would require a new contract. The studio, dazzled by the A&C success, agreed to tear up the contract and write another which would grant to Bud and Lou $150,000 per picture and twenty percent of the profits.

The Abbott and Costello phenomenon was observed at Metro-Goldwyn-Mayer, where Louis B. Mayer grew increasingly rancorous over the prize that had got away. He was convinced that the William Morris agency had committed Abbott and Costello to an M-G-M contract before they were signed by Universal. His anger surfaced when Universal tried to borrow an M-G-M contract player. "I'll never do business with you thieving bastards," Mayer responded.

Universal executives realized the danger of incurring the pique of Louie Mayer, indisputably the most powerful man in Hollywood. An arrangement was reached. M-G-M would be granted a picture a year with Abbott and Costello at the same terms of their Universal contract. But M-G-M balked at paying a percentage of the profits; the studio gave that privilege to no star, not even Clark Gable. So it was agreed that $150,000 would be paid to Bud and Lou and an additional $150,000 to Universal Pictures.

Lou was pleased to be returning as star to the studio where he had once worked as laborer and stunt man. But, although the budgets of the M-G-M pictures were triple those at Universal, Bud and Lou were treated as interlopers. Their first vehicle was a remake of the old Ziegfeld musical, *Rio Rita*, filmed with Bert Wheeler and Robert Woolsey at RKO in 1929. The story was updated and bolstered with John Grant's routines, and new songs were added for a Mayer protégé, Kathryn Grayson. Pandro Berman produced the film and S. Sylvan Simon directed, but both seemed uninterested. For all its M-G-M gloss, *Rio Rita* proved less entertaining than the earthy, economical comedies at Universal.

Having performed as guest stars for Kate Smith and Edgar

Bergen and on summer replacement shows, Bud and Lou were obviously ready for a radio series of their own. Eddie Sherman negotiated a contract with the William Esty agency for Bud and Lou to be sponsored by Camel cigarettes on NBC Thursday nights. The salary would be $20,000 a week. The contract required a delicate negotiation with Universal, since Bud and Lou would need to be released from filming every Thursday at noon. The studio acquiesced.

The Abbott and Costello Program had its debut on October 8, 1941, with Veronica Lake as guest star, Ken Niles as announcer, Connie Haines as singer, and Leith Stevens conducting the orchestra. Early each week, the show's producer, Don Bernard, brought the scripts to Universal for a brief review with Bud and Lou. Rehearsal began at one o'clock Thursday and continued through the afternoon, with a couple of run-throughs. Bud was generally acquiescent, but Lou was always questioning the material, particularly if he had never heard the jokes before. He wanted to be sure they were reliable. As he read along, he

The radio show often featured singers

would say, "That gag don't sound funny to me." The writer who supplied the line replied, "It got a big laugh on Fred Allen last week." "Okay, we'll use it," said Lou.

The programs were first-class productions, employing such guests as Humphrey Bogart, Van Johnson, Hedy Lamarr, Cary Grant, Alan Ladd, George Raft, John Garfield, and Betty Grable. In fact, the quality in radio seemed greater than what Bud and Lou were accustomed to in films. The comedy remained much the same, relying in large part on the routines that had served Bud and Lou well from their earliest burlesque days. Such as the Hertz U-Drive:

Bud: Now we'll have to rent a car.

Lou: Where can we get one?

Bud: At U-Drive.

Lou: Me drive?

Bud: No, U-Drive.

Lou: I said I'd drive.

Bud: You don't drive it. *I* drive it.

Lou: You drive what?

Bud: A U-Drive.

Lou (perplexed): Why should I drive when you want to drive?

Bud: Look, Costello, I'm renting a U-Drive and *I* drive it.

Lou: Oh, then we *both* drive.

Bud: No, we do nothing of the kind. When I say U-Drive, I don't mean "you drive." I mean that *I* drive although it's a U-Drive.

Lou (striving to understand): When you say you drive, you don't mean me drive?

Bud: No.

Lou: You mean you drive because I don't drive?

Bud: Now you got it.

Lou: I got it? *I don't even know what I'm talking about!* . . .

The movies, the radio show, and personal appearances brought Bud and Lou unimaginable treasure, and they began to live and spend as if it would never stop. And they gambled. The pastime of their burlesque years became their obsession now that they were Hollywood stars. They gambled compulsively, incessantly, almost demonically, spending more studio time over playing cards than they did in front of the camera. As soon as Arthur Lubin said, "Cut! Print!" they raced to one of their trailers and started dealing. Usually it was seven-card stud poker, at $10 a card and up. Most of the time Bud and Lou played alone, and that was good, because they were equal players. Both bad. Neither had the gambler's sense of figuring the percentages; their careers had turned so incredibly lucky, they believed that luck would extend to cards. Nothing could persuade them otherwise. With a pair of sevens in his hand, Lou would double the bet against a hand with three queens showing. Bud had a long history of failed inside straights. They played against each other with a kind of veiled violence, slapping down cards as if they were exchanging blows. Lou was exultant when he won, and he demanded immediate payment at the end of the match. Bud peeled off the bills from the roll of hundreds he always carried. He, too, insisted on cash when he beat Lou.

Sometimes they tired of playing against each other and sought another hand in the game. Eddie Sherman played with them, much against his will; he always left after a half-hour, declaring that he had to return to his office and attend to Abbott and Costello business. Whenever their producer, Alex Gottlieb, visited the movie set, Bud and Lou tried to enlist him in a game. He resisted. He had a gambler's sense, and he recognized what miserable players Bud and Lou were. To win from them offered little sport, and it could shatter their relationship. "No, fellas, I gotta get back to the office," he always told them.

One night Bud, Lou, Gottlieb, and their wives attended a birthday party at John Grant's house. As soon as the festivities were over, Lou suggested, "Let's play some poker." John Grant agreed, and there was no need to persuade Bud. Only Gottlieb demurred. "Look, Lou," he said, "I've watched you and Bud play. I don't want to take your money." Lou continued to urge him, finally turning on his little-boy smile and saying, "I won't

The eternal gin rummy game

show up at the studio tomorrow if you don't play." Gottlieb recognized that the threat was real. He sat down to play. Within a half-hour he had won $200, and he insisted on leaving.

Bud and Lou reported to work the following morning; it was their fourth week on *Pardon My Sarong*. Gottlieb visited the set in the morning, finding Bud and Lou in the midst of a poker game. "Sit down and play with us," Lou said. Again Gottlieb tried to resist, but he recognized the threatening glance from Lou.

"All right," the producer said. "I'll play until I lose two hundred dollars. That's all." They dealt a few hands until Bud and Lou were called into the scene. Gottlieb returned to his office.

Lou was on the telephone soon afterwards: "Hey, Alex, come back to the set. We got forty-five minutes before the next setup; let's play some more."

Like a teacher with a fractious pupil, Gottlieb explained, "I'm in conference with the writers about the next picture. You

The Abbotts at home

Bud (above, right) *with the kids, Bud Jr. and Rae Victoria*

Lou with wife Anne and daughters Patty and Carole (Christine had not yet arrived on the scene)

*The phrase was already
famous: Merle Oberon
(left) helps keep it
that way*

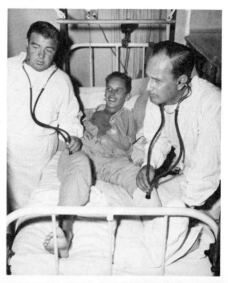

*Doing their bit for wounded GIs...
and selling War Bonds*

know the studio wants to go with it right away, Lou. I can't walk out and go down there to play cards with you guys. After all, I'm working for Universal." To his surprise, Lou did not insist.

A few minutes later, Cliff Work, the studio manager, was on the telephone. "Alex, we got a problem," said Work.

"What's that, Cliff?"

"Lou Costello just called me. He said that if Alex Gottlieb doesn't come down to Stage Fifteen and play cards with him and Bud, he's going to leave the studio right now."

"Cliff, I'm right in the middle of a script session for *Who Done It?* Isn't that more important than playing poker with two actors?"

"Alex, how much of this picture have you shot?"

"About three quarters."

"How can we release it without the other quarter?"

"I don't want to play cards with Bud and Lou. The only way I'll do it is if you order me to."

"This is an order."

Alex Gottlieb marched to Stage 15 and sat down to play seven-card stud. At Lou's insistence, Gottlieb returned to the game every day for the two weeks remaining of production. Each time the producer won, each time he was paid in cash, his total reaching $15,000. On the final day of filming, Gottlieb finished $2,000 ahead. But instead of paying off, Lou said, "We'll put it in the notebook." Later Lou declined to pay, declaring, "You've won enough already."

"That's fine," said Gottlieb, who wanted freedom more than the $2,000. "Now I don't have to play with you anymore." That rankled Lou. He stormed into Cliff Work's office to decree that he didn't want Alex Gottlieb to produce the next picture. He later relented, sending the message to Gottlieb through Work: "If we settle for a thousand dollars, will he play with us again?" Gottlieb remained as producer, but he would never play cards with Bud and Lou again.

Arthur Lubin did not remain as director of the Abbott and Costello movies. He had served them well in the first five starring films at Universal, drawing out the most attractive sides of their personalities and instilling as much class as the miserly budgets would permit. A man of some dignity, he tolerated their antics, such as when Bud and Lou presented him with a handsome piece of luggage; it fell open—and out tumbled hundreds of condoms. Lubin grew less tolerant of their work habits, particularly with Lou's reluctance to do more than one take. "That's good enough," Lou said after the first take, and he rushed off to the trailer and the poker game. He particularly disliked repeating John Grant's routines, with the result that Lubin had to film them with three cameras to achieve the proper angles (thus anticipating the common practice for television comedy). Finally Lubin said "No more," and Universal found others to direct Bud and Lou. They were B picture directors with roots in silent comedy—Earl C. Kenton, Jean Yarbrough, Charles Lamont.

When Bud and Lou first came to California for *One Night in the Tropics*, they lodged at the Knickerbocker Hotel in Hollywood, a favored stopping place for show people. When their movie future was assured with the Universal contract, Bud moved first into a rented place called the Dalton Ranch, then to a small house on Alcove Street in the San Fernando Valley, finally to a ranch-showplace on Woodley Avenue. Lou rented a home on Crescent Drive in Beverly Hills, then bought a house on a commercial acre at 4121 Longridge Avenue in the Valley. Of course, both Bud and Lou would live in the Valley—not only because of the proximity to Universal, but because they were burlesque people and would feel unwelcome in Beverly Hills.

Lou paid $13,500 for the modest house and acre, acquired an adjacent acre for $5,000. Then he started to build. A second floor was added. Daughters Patricia and Carole Lou each had a suite, the bathrooms equipped with large and small toilets, side by side, for nanny and child. The obligatory swimming pool, then the playroom–movie theater. Lou delighted in showing visitors around the place, demonstrating all the gadgets and appliances. He even designed a family flag—the motif was "4-C" (for the four Costellos) in white on a blue field—which he raised on the flagpole each morning and lowered each night. When Anne became pregnant in 1942, Lou began construction of an elaborate nursery, which he insisted on decorating in blue. He was certain that God would send him what he wanted most, a son.

Lou discovered what was for him a highly satisfactory way of furnishing his ever-growing estate.

Earl Kenton had been directing a garden sequence in *Hit the Ice*, and he arrived on the stage one morning to find the set stripped of its wrought-iron furniture. He called the prop man, who was perplexed about the disappearance. Kenton telephoned the producer, Alex Gottlieb: "I'm supposed to shoot some party stuff this morning, and I can't. All the furniture is gone."

"What do you mean, gone?" Gottlieb said.

"That's it—gone. Nobody knows where. We've checked all over the lot."

"But a stage full of furniture doesn't just disappear—wait a minute, I've got an idea." Gottlieb called Cliff Work and told the studio manager the situation, adding, "I think I know where the furniture might be."

Gottlieb telephoned Lou at home. "How does the wrought-iron furniture look in your back yard?" the producer asked.

"What do you mean?" Lou demanded.

"You know what I mean, Lou. I'll bet you five-to-one the furniture from our set is at your house."

Pause. "You're right, it's in my back yard, and it looks great, and it's gonna stay there."

Gottlieb's persuasion didn't work. He telephoned Cliff Work and proposed a solution: Lou could have the furniture if he would return it until the *Hit the Ice* sequence was completed. Universal agreed, and Lou loaned the studio its furniture.

The incident didn't end the looting of the Universal props. He was encouraged. Whenever Lou saw something on a set that might look good in his house, he took it. Once he was asked why. "Look," he answered, "when I no longer have any value to Universal, they're gonna piss on me. I'm getting everything I can—now!"

Yet neither Lou nor Bud seemed motivated by avarice. As in all other things, they seemed to be in a competition to prove which was the more generous. Dozens of movie people still working in the studios own gold money-clips and cufflinks, diamond-ornamented watches and bracelets enscribed from Bud or Lou. Their end-of-the-picture and Christmas gifts were incredibly lavish. Joe Kenny, assistant director on most of the Abbott and Costello pictures, was an affable man who could cajole the two stars into leaving their poker game for a scene with a brisk, "Come on, let's cut out the horseshit and get to work." One of his duties before each scene was to take Bud's diamond ring from his little finger, since the jewelry wouldn't fit the character he was playing. Joe carried the ring on his own finger, then returned it when Bud emerged from the set. At the finish of one of the pictures, Bud presented Joe with a small box. Inside was a gold ring with JOE spelled in diamonds.

Glen Adams, still photographer on the Abbott and Costello movies, arrived at the Longridge house one day to photograph Lou and the new construction. Lou insisted that they have a drink first, and he poured Adams a generous portion of scotch. Scotch was rare in wartime, and Adams remarked how good it tasted. When he finished taking the photographs, he returned to his car and found a case of the scotch he had enjoyed. Once he admired a sport shirt that Lou was wearing. On the following day, a member of Lou's retinue presented Adams with a dozen of the twenty-five-dollar sport shirts. To avoid embarrassment, the photographer learned never to praise anything that Lou possessed.

Bud and Lou were equally generous with their talents. During six weeks off from filming, they traveled the country playing movie houses, donating their salaries to the Army Emergency Relief Fund. In the summer they returned to the Atlantic City Steel Pier, the start of their advance into the big time. Their weekly salary for stage appearances was $10,000, but they told Frank Elliott they wouldn't charge him that much. Name a price, said Elliott. The answer: $1 a day.

Lou stopped in Paterson to see old friends and he was visited by his parish priest. After the warm reunion, the priest asked if Lou would buy a couple of dollar raffle tickets. Lou inquired about the raffle and learned that it was being held to finance the repair of the roof on St. Anthony's church. Lou inspected the building and said that a neighborhood raffle wouldn't be enough to pay for repairs. "Tear up the raffle tickets and leave it to me," he told the priest. Lou assigned Eddie Sherman to line up important entertainers for a St. Anthony's benefit in the eight-thousand-seat sports arena in Paterson. Bud and Lou, Kate Smith, Milton Berle, and other stars entertained in a spectacular show that raised $14,000 to repair St. Anthony's.

Bud and Lou did their act free for soldiers in army camps—and for the President in the White House. For all his sophistication, Franklin Roosevelt enjoyed the earthy humor of Abbott and Costello, especially "Who's on First?" which they performed for him on four occasions.

During a Washington visit Lou suggested that he and Bud attend the midnight show at the Gayety Theater for old time's sake. It was Washington's venerable burlesque house, where Bud and Lou had played many times and where Oliver Wendell Holmes, Jr., had been a regular patron. The owner, Colonel Jimmy Blake, was delighted to see his famous alumni and overjoyed when Bud and Lou offered to go onstage.

"On one condition," said Lou.

"What's that?" asked Blake.

"You put us on ahead of Maisie Dunn."

Colonel Blake introduced Bud and Lou to the thrilled audience just before the scheduled appearance of the star stripper, whom we will call Maisie Dunn. She had been notorious on the Mutual Wheel for her scorn of her fellow burlesque performers. They were generally a close-knit lot, sticking together for mutual protection. Maisie Dunn was concerned only with herself and her act, which was a masterpiece of erotic frenzy. She adored whipping her audience into a sexual high, removing her pasties and rubbing her nipples until the theater seemed in danger of a semen flood. She slithered through the curtain, then waited until the shouts of "More!" brought her return. Again and again she disappeared and came back, each time with a new bit of provocation.

106

One night when Bud and Lou were starting out as a team, she did such a performance as the two comics waited in the wings for their cue. She went back and forth through the curtains, the clamor rising to a high pitch. Finally she disappeared for the last time, ignoring the demands of her return. As she strode past the despairing Bud and Lou, she muttered, "Follow that, you pricks."

Lou never forgot. On the night of the triumphant return to the Gayety, he was in brilliant form. He milked the audience with every comic trick in his repertoire. He insisted on doing routine after routine until Bud was almost exhausted. When it appeared that the audience could laugh no more, Bud and Lou did "Who's on First?"

Finally they walked into the wings to tremendous applause. Waiting there was Maisie Dunn, clad in gossamer, G-string, pasties, and stage makeup. Lou smiled at her and said, "Follow that, you cunt."

11

Illness Strikes

WHAT A COURSE of events was set in motion when Bud and Lou departed on that war bond tour. It was early 1943, and the war had not yet turned for the United States and its allies; the Germans still held most of Europe and the Japanese most of the western Pacific. Bud and Lou were patriots, believers in the American dream. Were they not its proof, a couple of low comics who played before the President? Bud was too old to join the army, Lou had a weakened heart. They would serve where they could. The Secretary of the Treasury, Henry Morgenthau, called them personally and told them of the urgent need to sell war bonds. Taxes were not enough to finance the forces to invade Europe and press the war in the Pacific; citizens had to be convinced to lend their savings to the government. Would Bud and Lou be willing to barnstorm the country to sell war bonds? Of course they would.

For Lou it was a special sacrifice. On November 6, 1942, at Good Samaritan Hospital in Los Angeles, Anne gave birth by Caesarian section to their third child, a son. He was named Lou Costello, Jr., and such was his infant strength and vigor that his father nicknamed him Butch. Every morning before leaving for the studio, Lou visited the nursery to play with Butch, and he rushed home in the evening to see him again. He showed photographs to every visitor on his movie sets and reported each of the baby's new accomplishments. He was certain that Butch would accomplish his father's dream, to become a championship basketball player.

Leaving Butch was the toughest part of the war bond tour in February, 1943. Lou was unconcerned about the rigors of the trip—eighty-five cities to visit in thirty-eight days. He and Bud had performed a whole day and night of burlesque and caught the Midnight Flyer to the next town, had done twelve shows a a day at the Atlantic City Steel Pier, had played a Broadway matinee and evening performance, a radio broadcast, and a nightclub show, all in an eighteen-hour span. Despite his ample waistline, Lou still considered himself an athlete.

The war bond tour tested his strength. Sometimes army bombers flew them from city to city. Or state troopers sped them along highways, sirens screaming. Pat Costello followed their route in Lou's Packard, carrying the wardrobe. Bud and Lou scarcely had time to change shirts and gulp down coffee and doughnuts before they were rushed off to a war plant or city center to make their pitch. Audiences numbering 10,000 or 15,000 roared when Lou opened with the trademark of their radio show, "He-e-e-e-e-y, Abbott!" They engaged in local jokes, then delivered two or three of the routines. The pitch followed. Having sold burlesque comedy—without dirty jokes —to the toughest audiences in America, Bud and Lou were irresistible salesmen. They pleaded, they cajoled, they cited the boys in the foxholes and on the carriers far at sea, they talked of apple pie and Mom, they invited everyone to sing "God Bless America."

"All right, neighbors, we're going to divide the audience in half," Bud announced. "I'll take this side—the bankers."

Lou remarked, "I'll take the other side—the crapshooters. Now we'll see whose side will win. How about it, crapshooters, can we beat those bankers? Who'll go for a thousand-dollar bond?"

The bidding began, with pretty girls moving through the audience to accept the pledges. When the last twenty-five-dol-lar bond was sold, Bud and Lou rewarded the citizens' generosity with "Who's on First?" Then they climbed into the state troopers' car and sped to the next city, Pat Costello trailing in the Packard with fresh sets of clothes.

The 1943 winter was punishingly cold, and Bud and Lou raced from frigid streets to overheated auditoriums. Sometimes they auctioned their own clothes for bond pledges and ended the performance doing "Who's on First?" in their underwear. In Boston a dozen adolescent boys appeared at the hotel and asked Bud and Lou to attend a savings-stamp rally they were having in their neighborhood. Bud and Lou went.

The last stop was New York City, and it included a visit to a nearby army camp. Bud and Lou did their show outdoors in subfreezing weather, and when Lou returned to the hotel he told Bud, "I'm burning up. Get me a doctor." The doctor said Lou might have influenza and suggested that he enter a hospital.

"No, I'm going home," Lou insisted. "I gotta see Butch." He and Bud took the train across the country, and Lou never left his room. When he arrived at Union Station in Los Angeles, Anne and his parents were awaiting him. They were shocked at how pale he looked. Papa Cristillo and Lou always kissed when they met, but this time Lou backed away. "Don't come near me, Papa," Lou said. "I don't know what I've got, but I sure don't want to give it to you. I'm in terrific pain." Lou went home to view Butch asleep in the nursery; he was astonished by how much the baby had grown in six weeks. Lou watched until he could stand no longer, then he went to bed.

The doctors came and went, shaking their heads and murmuring together in the hallway. The patient had a constant fever and swelling in the joints. The most alarming symptom of all was the erratic behavior of his heart. The diagnosis was rheumatic fever, normally a children's disease but sometimes attacking young adults. The gravest danger was the damage that it could do to the heart—damage that might not be manifested until years afterward. Lou would need total rest.

It was a frightening time for Lou. He had never known a serious illness in his thirty-seven years; now, with himself and Bud the top box-office stars in the country, everything stopped. He could do nothing, not even play with Butch. He had no fear about money; it still poured in from the profits on the Universal pictures. But the doctors gave no assurance that Lou could ever work again. Lou realized that a prolonged absence from the screen would be ruinous. The hotter the stars, the faster they cooled down.

For Bud it was a bewildering time. He still bore resentment over Lou's high-handed imposition of the 60–40 split of their movie earnings. Yet Bud's affection for the little guy ran deep. Bud carried on with the radio show for a couple of weeks, then he announced that he didn't have the heart to continue without his partner, and the show was suspended.

Lou was cheered by the outpouring of thousands of get-well messages from fans. Many Hollywood stars came to visit him, including his boyhood idol, Charlie Chaplin; in a public statement, Chaplin had proclaimed Lou the funniest comic working in films. Lou was forbidden to play cards, but that didn't stop him from gambling. He invented a game to play with his doctor, Guess the Blood Pressure. Dr. Victor Kovner estimated Lou's blood pressure, then Lou tried to prove him wrong, employing mental attitudes to push it up or down. They also bet on the nurse's temperature, but Lou accused the doctor of cheating by having the nurse leave the room to put ice or hot water in her mouth.

The recovery was exasperatingly slow. He was told that if he got up before the fever had completely subsided the damage to his heart could be fatal. As soon as the weather grew warm enough, he asked to have his bed moved outdoors. There he could watch Butch play in his crib and Pat and Carole Lou swim in the pool. He gave an interview on the terrace four months after the attack and talked of his plan to work for a foundation to help rheumatic fever sufferers, as the March of Dimes had done for victims of infantile paralysis.

"I never knew how many people suffered from rheumatic fever," he told the reporter. "My mail has been full of letters from patients, mostly children and young people, who read about my illness. I know how much care my own case has involved, and I know that most patients aren't in a position to get the same kind of care." Lou said he had discussed his plan for a foundation with Bud Abbott, and they planned to give shows to raise funds to benefit rheumatic fever victims from all walks of life.

The weeks in bed continued, causing grave concern to the National Broadcasting Company, for which *The Abbott and Costello Program* was a mainstay of its Thursday night schedule, and especially for Universal Pictures Corporation, which had been restored to solvency by the Abbott and Costello movies. The bedside visitors became fewer as Lou's illness continued, but always there was Eddie Sherman, arriving each day to report on the latest checks from Universal and to convey the Hollywood gossip. From his bed he could see Sherman drive up Longridge in his pea-green Cadillac convertible. "What a beautiful car!" Lou often said. "I'd love to get a car like that." Eddie made a deal with Lou: on the first day that he got out of bed, Lou would have the car. Finally, on a happy day in November, Eddie signed over the pink slip for the Cadillac to Lou.

12

"Let's Just Do the Best Goddamn Show"

NOVEMBER 4, 1943, the longest day of Lou Costello's life.

He awoke early, savoring the pleasure of rising from bed without the pain stabbing at his chest. He walked to the nursery, and for a half hour father and son played on the carpet with blocks, balls, and the rest of the boy's vast collection of toys. Lou was astounded by the strength and alertness of Butch, two days shy of his first birthday but seeming much older. Lou promised him the biggest first-birthday party the town had ever seen.

Lou spent the morning in rising anticipation of his first return to work in nine months. The doctors had pronounced him well enough to resume the radio show, and he read and reread the script, changing lines and underlining others for emphasis. Pat Costello arrived at one o'clock to drive Lou to NBC studios in Eddie Sherman's pea-green Cadillac. Lou kissed Butch good-bye, then Pat and Carole and Anne. "Now I want you to keep Butch up for the show," Lou told his wife. "I want to see if he recognizes his daddy's voice."

Pat Costello drove along Ventura Boulevard, over the Cahuenga Pass and down Vine Street to Sunset Boulevard, turning into the NBC parking lot. "Welcome back, Mr. Costello," said the studio guard. Again and again Lou was stopped in the halls as stars, musicians, script girls, and pages greeted his re-

Lou Costello's greatest joy and greatest sorrow: Nobody loved a son more. After being on his back for six months, Lou (right) takes his first steps with Lou Jr.

Lou between his parents; Anne is on Bud's right

turn. Inside Studio D, there were warm reunions with his producer, Martin Gosch; the announcer, Ken Niles; vocalist Connie Haines; and other regulars on the show. Lou sat down for the first reading with Bud and the rest of the cast and the guest star, Lana Turner, a replacement for Veronica Lake, who was ill. The rehearsal went well. Lou seemed subdued, but he always held back in rehearsal, saving his punch for the performance.

Watching the rehearsal with vast satisfaction was Eddie Sherman. About four o'clock, an NBC page tapped him on the shoulder and said, "You have a phone call, Mr. Sherman. It's urgent." Sherman went to the control booth and lifted the receiver. Anne Costello was on the other end, sobbing hysterically. "It's Butch—he fell in the pool," she said.

"How is he?" Sherman asked.

"I—I don't know. He's not moving. The firemen are working on him now."

"Do you have help?"

"Yes. Marie is here, and some neighbors. How can we tell Lou?"

"You leave that to me. Now just hold on, Anne, and I'll get Lou there just as fast as I can."

Sherman put down the telephone and gazed through the control booth window at Lou as he clowned with Lana Turner. Sherman walked to the side of the stage and beckoned to Lou. Lou shook his head, indicating that he was in rehearsal. His face stolid, his manner urgent, Sherman again beckoned for Lou to leave the stage.

"For Chrissake, Eddie, you're interruptin' me with a beautiful broad," Lou remarked.

"Lou, I want you to come with me," Sherman said gravely.

"You mean leave rehearsal?" Lou asked.

"Yes."

Lou realized from Eddie's manner that he had to leave. On the way out of the studio, Eddie whispered to Bud, "I'm taking Lou home. There's been an accident with the baby. If it's as bad as I think it is, Lou won't be back. Better tell NBC to have another star standing by."

Lou was silent as he followed Sherman to the parking lot. As they got into the car, Lou finally asked, "Where are you taking me?"

"You gotta come with me; that's all I'm telling you," Sherman answered. He drove up Vine Street, turned on Yucca, then Cahuenga, and started driving toward the Valley.

"Something happened to my kid!" Lou exclaimed. "You're taking me home!"

"That's right, Lou," Sherman said. "The baby fell in the pool. The fire department is working on him now. Anne just called me. That's all she said."

As they turned the corner on Longridge, they could see the fire truck driving away from the house. Lou rushed inside and looked out to the pool. Beside it the tiny figure was covered with a sheet. Lou was too stunned to weep.

"What happened?" he asked his sister Marie. She told him that Anne had put Butch in the playpen beside the pool at 2:30. She went inside to answer the telephone and when she returned, Butch was gone; he was so strong that he had broken out of the playpen. Anne looked in the pool and found him floating face-down in a foot and a half of water. She pulled him out and screamed for help. Two neighbor women came running; one tried artificial respiration on the baby, the other called the fire department. Butch failed to respond to the inhalator, and the family doctor, Victor Kovner, pronounced him dead.

Anne was frenzied with grief. So were Lou's parents and Anne's mother, and Dr. Kovner gave them sedatives. Lou suppressed his sorrow. He stood silently beside the swimming pool, gazing into the blue water, then retired to his office with only Harry Abbott as companion; Lou loved and respected Bud's older brother.

Eddie Sherman knocked on the door. "Lou, NBC has been calling. Jimmy Durante said he'll go on for you tonight. Red Skelton and Bob Hope, too, and Mickey Rooney."

"You tell NBC that I'm coming down to do the show," Lou replied.

"Do you think you'd be able to?" the manager asked.

He nodded. "I told Anne to keep the baby up so he could hear me. Wherever Butch is tonight, I'm going to do the show for him."

Sherman drove Lou back to Hollywood, and they arrived at Studio D a half-hour before broadcast time. Bud Abbott embraced his partner, but Lou brushed aside sympathy. "Let's just do the best goddamn show we've ever done," Lou said.

Ken Niles did the warm-up of the audience, which included twenty-five rheumatic fever patients—Lou's guests from the naval hospital at Corona. None of the audience was aware of the tragedy that had befallen Lou. He stood before the microphone with a lighted cigar, only the shaking of his script betraying his emotion to the rest of the cast. The director counted down the seconds, then Leith Stevens' orchestra began the theme music. Ken Niles announced breathlessly: "The Abbott and Costello Program for Camel cigarettes, starring Bud Abbott and Lou Costello, with their guest star, the glamorous Lana Turner, the rhythms of Leith Stevens and his orchestra, the swinging, singing Connie Haines, yours truly, Ken Niles, and now——"

Lou bellowed, "He-e-e-e-e-y, Abbott!"

"I just took a shower with my shirt, socks, and underwear on," said Lou.

"Now why did you do that, Costello?" Bud demanded.

"Do you know a better way of getting your laundry done?" They did other jokes concerning wartime shortages and lack of services and made references to Lou's health, the studio audience and those listening at home being aware that the broadcast was his first after the long illness. During the band numbers and commercials, Lou slumped into a chair. But as soon as the director pointed his finger from the control booth, he was back at the microphone for his cue. Once he faltered. He read the line, "I feel sad today." With a single beat more than he ordinarily would have taken, he added, "I broke up with my girl today." The show continued, Bud enforcing the usual staccato pace, although Lana Turner was so distraught she could scarcely deliver her lines above a whisper.

Finally the last inane joke was broadcast to the nation's listeners, and Lou tossed his script to a uniformed WAVE in the front row. Ken Niles introduced Bud.

"Thanks, Ken," Bud said. "Ladies and gentlemen, now that our program is over and we have done our best to entertain you, I would like to take a moment to pay tribute to my best friend, and to a man who has more courage than I have ever seen displayed in the theater. Tonight the old expression, 'The show must go on,' was brought home to all of us on this program more clearly than ever before. Just a short time before our broadcast started, Lou Costello was told that his baby—one year old in two days—had died. In the face of the greatest tragedy which can come to any man, Lou Costello went on tonight so that you, the radio audience, would not be disappointed. There is nothing more that I can say except that I know all join me in expressing our deepest sympathy to a great trouper. Good night."

There were sobs in the studio audience. After a three-minute silence, the crowd filed out of the studio, and Lou went home.

Is there anything in human experience more heartbreakingly sad than a child's funeral? This was the ordeal that faced Anne and Lou, and they had to endure it not only amid their own families and friends, but under the gaze of the nation as well. It seemed almost too much to bear, and Anne showed evidence of breaking as she visited her child at the mortuary. She had brought young Lou's first pair of hard-soled shoes, purchased for the funeral, and for long minutes she tied and retied the strings, repeating, "This one I always called my angel."

Anne and Lou sat together at the requiem high mass in their parish church, St. Francis de Sales, and Anne sobbed as she stared at the tiny casket on the altar. Lou also seemed overcome with grief, but both he and Anne found solace in the priest's words: "God figured that Mr. and Mrs. Costello had everything, so he called their only son to be an angel."

118

The wound never healed, not for Anne, not for Lou. Neither would be the same afterward. Lou could never truly forgive Anne for what he felt was her negligence that resulted in Butch's death. Anne always felt the guilt. Underlying their lives ever afterward was the indescribable sorrow of those brief moments at the swimming pool on November 4, 1943.

13

Back to Work

WORK to be done, wounds to be healed. Everyone agreed that the best remedy for Lou's sorrow would be for him to get busy again. He himself was eager for a return to films. The Abbott and Costello movies had been appearing at the rate of four a year; because of Lou's illness, he and Bud would be off the screen a full year. Both Universal and M-G-M wanted to market a new Abbott and Costello film lest the vogue for their comedy diminish. M-G-M had first call, and the studio devised a pastiche to make use of the sets created for *Kismet*, starring Ronald Colman and Marlene Dietrich. Gag writers Harry Ruskin and Harry Crane, together with the omnipresent John Grant, fashioned a script that was called *Lost in a Harem*. The director was Chuck Riesner, an M-G-M oldtimer who had once assisted Charlie Chaplin. Riesner worked with incredible speed, and his methods were to spoil Lou ever afterward.

Universal was eager to beat M-G-M to the nation's theaters with the return of Abbott and Costello. The studio's hopes were upset by the loss of its A&C expert, Alex Gottlieb.

After *Hit the Ice*, Gottlieb had left Universal for a contract as a producer at Warner Brothers. He had become disenchanted with Lou's attitude toward his work. "I'm as good as Chaplin or Lloyd," Lou insisted, and he believed that anything

Lou with Charlie Chaplin

he said was funny. Gottlieb tried to explain that Chaplin and Lloyd had planned their comedy with meticulous care. Lou was convinced that he could work instinctively, and he rarely would submit to more than one take. Often he said, "Keep 'em rolling," and moved on to the next scene. Gottlieb found Lou upsetting in other ways. For *Who Done It?* the producer had cast William Bendix, who had appeared in a string of Broadway failures and had recently played a small role in the Katharine Hepburn–Spencer Tracy film, *Woman of the Year*. Gottlieb hired Bendix to play the dumb detective, Brannigan. Bendix had one key scene in *Who Done It?* in which Lou tricked Brannigan into handcuffing himself. On the day it was filmed, Lou thundered into Gottlieb's office and warned, "Don't you ever do that to me again!"

"Do what to you, Lou?" the producer asked.

"Don't you ever put anybody who's funnier than me in a picture of mine!"

That contributed to Gottlieb's decision to leave Universal

121

and the Abbott and Costello films. But mainly he realized that two stars who had risen so fast must necessarily face a precipitous decline. If Gottlieb remained as their producer, he would surely suffer the same fate.

The new producer was Edmund Hartman, a Broadway songwriter who had turned to film comedy. He was told to prepare a script in the swiftest possible time so Universal could be the first with the return to the screen of Abbott and Costello. Hartman, Hal Fimberg, and John Grant wrote the screenplay of *In Society* with material from an old burlesque hand, Sid Fields. Hartman believed he could meet the Universal deadline if the movie could be filmed with dispatch. He didn't realize how much dispatch Lou had in mind.

"Bud and I just finished a picture at M-G-M and we found out how to work," Lou announced at the first production meeting. "We come in at ten and we leave at three. We don't rehearse, we do a scene once, and if the director don't get it, that't too bad. We move on to the next scene."

Hartman and the director, Jean Yarbrough, were appalled. Perhaps M-G-M, with its coddling of stars, could manage with such techniques, but that wasn't the system at Universal. Lou would not be dissuaded. He kept regular hours, but he rarely entertained more than a single take, and he sought shortcuts wherever possible. Hartman and his fellow writers were constantly readjusting the script to accommodate Lou's whims. One day he announced, "We're gonna do Floogle Street in this picture." Hartman argued that the famed burlesque routine had nothing whatsoever to do with the plot of *In Society*.

"That's all right; we're gonna do Floogle Street," Lou insisted. And so John Grant hastily wrote a cinematic version, changing the name to Beagle Street. Lou cast his friends and relatives, selected a street set on the backlot and directed the action himself. Yarbrough photographed the routine in one take with three cameras, and Hartman simply inserted the scene into the continuity without an explanation. It made no less sense than anything else in the picture. With three weeks remaining on the schedule, Lou announced to the producer: "If there's

122

anything you really need for the picture, you better get it before Wednesday." Hartman asked him why. "Because I gotta go to New York Wednesday," Lou said. Hartman argued that important sequences were yet to be filmed. "Wednesday I leave," Lou insisted.

With sleepless nights of rewriting, Hartman managed to compress the remainder of the shooting into a few days. Lou cooperated fully, with one exception. Hartman had devised opening titles in which Bud and Lou would stick their heads through the O's in their last names. Lou arrived on the set and studied the backdrop painted with the words "Abbott and Costello In Society."

"The idea is that Bud and I are supposed to stick our heads out at the beginning of the picture?" Lou asked.

"That's right, Lou," the producer said. "We should get a good reaction from the audience, since you've been off the screen for a year."

"And Bud's head comes out first?" Lou asked.

"Yes, that's the way it reads—Abbott and Costello."

"Forget it. I'm not going to follow Abbott." He walked out the stage door and didn't return.

Hartman worked with three film editors to assemble *In Society* in time to beat M-G-M to the theaters. They made the deadline, and if Lou's intransigence damaged the plot, nobody noticed. At the first preview in Inglewood, the audience started laughing at the appearance of the Universal trademark. When "Abbott and Costello" flashed on the screen, there was a roar of laughter, and the laughs continued through the credits. The opening shot, an insert of a dripping faucet, evoked one of the loudest laughs Hartman had ever heard in a theater, and the remainder of the seventy-five minutes brought the same response. The Universal executives massaged their palms in happy recognition that Bud and Lou remained a magical draw.

14

The First Split

MUCH could be learned of the ebb and flow of personal fortunes at Universal Studio by studying the noontime happenings in the commissary. In the 1940s the Universal commissary was little different from the time it was built thirty years before by Uncle Carl Laemmle—except that there was no longer an entrance to the general public on Lankershim Boulevard. (Uncle Carl had earned a nice profit by allowing tourists to enter and observe the actors at feeding time.) The decor had changed little since that time, nor, some said, had the waitresses. The commissary was divided into three areas: the counter, where quick, cheap meals could be bought; the main dining room, with tables and slightly higher prices; the Sun Room, where the executives, producers, directors, and stars lunched on an exclusive menu. The Sun Room had its own social strata. The best tables near the windows were reserved for the studio's prestigious, independent producers, such as Walter Wanger and Mark Hellinger. Along the walls were tables at which the major stars could conduct press interviews or complain to their agents. Directors and less well-known actors sat within the flow of traffic. The main feature of the Sun Room was a large round table at which the studio executives sat. Reputations were made and nullified at that table. Maria Montez, in full Arabian Nights costume, had been known to sweep into the Sun Room, find the executive table empty, then retire to the women's room until her entrance mattered. The most feared fate was for an actor to be told by the hostess that a table in the Sun Room was not available; that could mean that his contract would not be renewed.

How did Bud and Lou fit into the pattern?

In the beginning, with *One Night in the Tropics*, they sat alone together in the main dining room, unknown amid bit players and cowboy extras. *Buck Privates* brought them promotion to the Sun Room, where they were sometimes joined by Eddie Sherman or a visiting friend from burlesque. Their table grew in size, Lou accompanied by his brother Pat and his brother-in-law Joe Kirk, and Bud by Charlie Murray, a New York friend who drove Bud's car, and nephew Norman Abbott. Lou always managed to be noticed. Once he arrived in the commissary with a three-piece band. He would shout a wisecrack across the room or perhaps leap up, grab a waitress, and dance her back to the kitchen.

As their success grew, Bud and Lou no longer lunched together; instead, they gathered their own sycophants separately, each table competing to produce the most laughter. The competition of Bud and Lou spread to other areas. Each seemed intent on building the bigger showplace. After Lou put up his playroom on Longridge, Bud erected on his Woodley property a building the size of a restaurant. It had a bar that stretched the entire length of the room; passersby sometimes dropped in and ordered drinks, believing the place to be a public tavern. And the oblivious Bud served them.

Lou put a large swimming pool in the backyard of his property; Bud built one that was longer. Bud bought a restaurant on Ventura Boulevard, the Backstage, where he could entertain his friends from burlesque. Lou purchased a night club on Fairfax Avenue, the Band Box. Lou invested in a yacht to take his family sailing on weekends. Bud rented a yacht, making sure it was six feet longer than Lou's.

In press interviews they maintained the same kind of contentious banter they performed on radio and in films. A magazine writer recorded the scene when Bud and Lou were being chased by a band of Indians. It was a process shot with the two comedians racing in a jalopy, which was being animated by grips (stagehands). Lou commented to Bud, "Fame! Think of going home and telling the kid, 'I jiggle the car for Costello and Abbott'!"

"*Abbott* and Costello," Bud corrected.

"An error in printin'," said Lou.

"Never mind. You lose your hat in this scene. Remember that."

"Why?"

"Just because you're dumb."

"Smart guys don't lose hats?"

"No."

"You're a smart guy?"

"Yes."

"So you're expectin' me to knock your hat off?"

"Yes." Bud threatened, "Why don't you?"

Lou, retreating, "I'm not so dumb." To the director: "He wants me to knock his hat off."

"I do not," said Bud.

"You said you were expectin' it."

"I said you were dumb."

"That's different."

After the scene was completed, Bud explained their success: "Corn, gentlemen, corn. Every gag guaranteed to be seven hundred years old."

"Myself," Lou declared, "I'm an artist."

"An artist?" Bud scoffed.

"I'm in pitchas. I'm a pitcha artist."

"Like Barrymore?"

"More like Boyer."

"You wouldn't like a nice push in the teeth, would you?"

"Who's askin'?"

"Me."

"I will take your offer under consideration."

Lou could display tenderness toward Bud, particularly on

126

the rare occasions when Bud suffered an epileptic seizure on the movie set. It was a harrowing experience for everyone who was present, and Lou helped get Bud out of view until the attack was over. At other times, however, Lou could be astonishingly cruel. He showed his Universal paycheck to workers on the set, bragging, "See—I get more than Bud does." Lou was delighted when fans berated Bud in public saying, "Why don't you stop picking on that little man?"

Bud used interviews to stress his own importance in the team. "Every comic needs a straight man, a 'lecturer,'" he once told me. "There are only seven original jokes in the world. It's the way you sell and deliver 'em that gets the laughs. One of the funniest men in the business could be that Shemp Howard, who was with the Three Stooges, but now is making lousy shorts. Why? No lecturer." Bud enjoyed demonstrating the straight man's importance by an exercise with interviewers. He instructed them, "No matter what I ask you, you give me any of three answers: 'Who,' 'What,' or 'I don't know.'" He then did a reverse version of the Baseball Routine that proved surprisingly funny.

"Lou is the funniest man in the world—when he wants to be," said Bud. "I trained for this job for a long time. I was in show business before Lou was born. I worked with many comics in burlesque, waiting for the right one to come along. When I saw Lou, I said, 'This is it!' I know every move of Lou's body; I know just how he is going to react. When we go out on the stage of the Roxy Theater in New York, we haven't decided what we'll do. Lou can choose from any of a thousand routines, and I'll have the questions for him."

Lou's temper flashed when he read such interviews, and his sarcasm to Bud increased. Bud responded instinctively; when a scene called for him to slap Lou, he did so with a fury that made set workers gasp. Lou clenched his fists to avoid hitting back. A hanger-on asked why Lou took such punishment. "If I ever hit Bud, it would destroy our whole relationship," Lou said. "It'll never seem the same again. I gotta be the little guy that gets slapped."

When the break came in 1945, it was over a triviality. The domestic staff at the Costello house came and went, and one of those who went was a maid named Minnie. Lou fired her. She found a position with Mickey Rooney and his mother, who had danced in burlesque with Betty Abbott. Betty sometimes visited Mickey's mother, and she was driven by Bud's chauffeur and butler, Smallwood Goff. He fell in love with Minnie and they were married. When a maid's job opened at the Abbott house, Smallwood suggested, "Why not hire Minnie?" The Abbotts agreed.

Lou was furious. He considered it a breach of friendship for Bud to hire a maid he had fired. He telephoned Bud and told him so. "I demand that you fire Minnie," Lou shouted.

"What the hell for?" Bud replied. "She's a good worker and she's married to Smallwood now."

"I don't care. I don't want her working for you, and that's final."

"That isn't final. It's a free country; she can work for anybody she wants to."

"Abbott, I'm warning you: either you fire Minnie or we're through. Understand?"

"I understand that you're making a mountain out of a molehill. Now just calm down."

"Don't tell me to calm down. Are you gonna fire her or aren't you?"

"Minnie stays here."

"Okay, you asked for it. I ain't never gonna work with you again."

Lou summoned Eddie Sherman and told him the news. "I've had it with that guy," Lou ranted. "I been carryin' him long enough. From now on I work alone. I don't need no straight man. And if I do, I can buy 'em a dime a dozen."

With his usual calm manner, Sherman tried to explain to Lou that he and Bud had contractual commitments with Universal and M-G-M for movies, with Camel Cigarettes for radio, with theaters around the country for personal appearances.

"I don't care," said Lou. "It's over. Take care of it, little man."

128

Sherman believed that Lou's anger would diminish with time, but it didn't. Lou's resolve firmed; the partnership was over. The news leaked to the press, and the A&C press agent, Joe Glaston, strove mightily to minimize the report. The difference merely concerned the new Abbott and Costello contract with Universal, Glaston claimed; Bud believed that Eddie Sherman should not be included in the deal, Lou felt he should. "The controversy is strictly a business rather than a personal matter," said Glaston, declaring that the contracts for films and radio would be fulfilled. Meanwhile, Bud and Lou were not talking to each other.

Fortunately for Glaston, Sherman and the myriad of others whose livelihoods depended on continuance of the partnership, the split came in the summer. The radio show was on vacation, and Bud and Lou were not scheduled to make another movie until the fall. But they did have theater appearances to fulfill, including an important one at the Roxy in New York. Lou agreed to keep the date only when Eddie Sherman argued that it would be suicidal not to.

The Roxy marquee carried the legend "THOSE MAD COMEDY MANIACS OF RADIO AND MOTION PICTURES—FUNNIER THAN YOU'VE EVER SEEN THEM BEFORE." Backstage there was comedy of a different kind. Whenever Lou had anything to communicate to Bud, he did so through his lawyer. Bud used his own lawyer to send messages to Lou. When the fanfare signaled their entrance onstage, Lou came from one wing, Bud from the opposite side—"Hi, Bud"; "Hi, Lou"—and off they went on one of their comedic fantasies. As soon as they had drained the jammed audience of laughter, they retreated to opposite sides of the stage, then back to their own dressing rooms.

The New York columnists maintained a barrage of items about the Abbott and Costello feud, alarming executives of Universal Pictures and the Camel radio sponsors. The rumors had to be stopped, and Bud agreed to make an explanation at a press conference. But when reporters arrived at his suite in the Hotel Astor, Bud wasn't there. Bud's attorney, Nate Friedman, and a Universal spokesman declared that Abbott and Costello would continue as a team at least for the twenty-six remaining

129

months of their Universal contract. Bud and Lou had been saying bad things about each other for a variety of reasons, the reporters were told. Actors are naturally temperamental; Bud and Lou had been working too hard; they had been made irritable by the New York heat; and they had become upset over columnists' remarks.

The reporters did not seem totally convinced. One of them appeared backstage at the Roxy to confront Bud and Lou. Both declared that their differences had been blown out of proportion, that they had reconciled and would continue working together. But the reporter noted that when the pair went to the elevator, they talked to chorus girls, not to each other. And when the elevator arrived at the dressing-room floor, Bud and Lou retired to their separate rooms without exchanging a word or a nod.

The next stop on the tour was Baltimore, and reporters were waiting for them. Bud and Lou arrived in separate train coaches and drove to the hotel in different limousines. They declined to answer questions about the feud. Would they pose for a photograph shaking hands? "Yeah, sure," said Lou. Bud shrugged. They shook hands.

The same chill prevailed in Philadelphia and at Atlantic City, where they played the Steel Pier without a breath of sentiment. They returned to California on different trains. They continued to communicate through Eddie Sherman, who bore messages from one camp to the other.

Lou now became afflicted with Chaplin's disease, a complaint that has infected all film comedians from Harry Langdon to Jerry Lewis. The major symptom is an irresistible desire to play pathos. Lou announced that for his next film he did not want to perform the usual routines with Bud Abbott. Instead he was going to play a believable character in a dramatic story with comedic overtones.

Universal was compliant. The Abbott and Costello pictures, which could always be counted on for a boost in income, were not drawing as well as they had in wartime. *The Naughty Nineties*, in which Bud and Lou performed "Who's on First?" had proved disappointing. M-G-M had done such indifferent business with *Abbott and Costello in Hollywood* that it dropped the option for further A&C films. The Universal committee concurred with Lou that a change was advisable—hence, *Little Giant*.

The script portrayed Lou as a country boy who went off to the city with ambitions of becoming a supersalesman. Bud played two minor roles, as a sales manager and his own cousin. Lou demanded that the studio hire a first-class director for the film, and William Seiter agreed to direct *Little Giant* at $100,000, half the cost of early Abbott and Costello films. He had directed Laurel and Hardy in *Sons of the Desert*, the Marx Brothers in *Room Service*, as well as portions of *If I Had a Million*, *Roberta* and *Broadway*. Ordinarily an amiable man, Seiter was irritated by Lou's unwillingness to rehearse and his insistence on only one take. "Okay, I'll fix the little bastard," the director muttered. "I'll direct the picture exactly as it appears in the script, every line, every stage direction." He did, thus depriving *Little Giant* of the improvisation and spontaneity that comedy directors can contribute to films.

Lou continued his campaign for change with *The Time of Their Lives*. No Abbott and Costello routines; in fact, Bud and Lou appeared together only briefly. That, too, was part of Lou's scheme, since he was still at odds with Bud despite their public declarations of solidarity. With *The Time of Their Lives*, a fantasy of a Revolutionary era tinker who returned as a ghost in 1946, Bud and Lou were blessed with a sympathetic director, Charles Barton, small in size, a former vaudevillian and movie prop man who understood the workings of film comedy. It was the beginning of a long, fruitful, and mostly harmonious association.

A period of disharmony began one night after *The Time of Their Lives* had been filming for three weeks. Barton received a telephone call from Lou at home. "I'm not coming to work tomorrow," Lou announced.

"Why not? Are you sick?" the director asked.

"No, I'm not sick. I just realized what's wrong with the script."

"What's that?"

"I'm playing the wrong part. I should be playing Bud's part and he should play mine. I want to switch."

"Lou, are you crazy? We'd have to scrap three weeks of shooting."

"That's the way I want it, Charlie. Either I switch roles or I don't show. Good night."

Lou didn't appear the following day, nor the day after. For two weeks he remained absent while Barton and Universal played a risky game of calling his bluff. Then one day Lou appeared at the studio, resumed his role, and completed the picture without further incident and with no explanation.

Contact between Bud and Lou remained minimal. They were together only when necessary for their movie and radio duties; they had abandoned their between-the-scenes card games. Then something remarkable happened. Before the dispute over the sacked maid, Bud and Lou had decided to finance the cost of a community center for children in the Hollenbeck district of east Los Angeles, a poor section without recreational op-portunities. They continued with the plan despite their disaf-fection, agreeing to a theater tour to benefit the center. At a meeting to discuss the tour, they remained distant and cool until Bud remarked, "Why don't we name the place after your kid, Lou?"

"What's that?" said Lou, taken by surprise.

"Why don't we call it the Lou Costello, Jr., Youth Founda-tion?"

"Gee, that's a swell idea, Bud," said Lou, the tears forming in his eyes.

The feud was over, for a time.

15

The World and A&C at Peace–For a Time

THE YEAR was 1946, and the world was at peace after fifteen bloody years. The failed League of Nations closed its doors in Geneva and transferred its effects to the new and hopeful United Nations, then meeting in its first General Assembly. The victors tried and hanged a host of archvillains, from Joachim von Ribbentrop and Josef Kramer, the Beast of Belsen, to General Yamashita and Karl Hermann Frank, who ordered the destruction of Lidice. America was growing fond of its peppery president, Harry Truman, although the loss of F.D.R. was still felt by everyone. Soldiers and sailors were still returning from abroad, and the colleges were beginning to fill up with veterans seeking new lives with the help of the G.I. Bill of Rights.

Business was good, the factories working at full steam to provide cars and appliances that were scarce during the war, builders throwing up new cities to house the veterans and their new families. The movie business was good, too. Returning veterans like Clark Gable, James Stewart, Tyrone Power, Gene Kelly, Henry Fonda, and David Niven brought renewed vitality to the screen, and Americans had money to spend for theater tickets. The movie of the year seemed to say it all–*The Best Years of Our Lives*.

Amid the movie prosperity one company was in distress:

Universal Pictures. The committee of theater men who ran the studio had relied on the Abbott and Costello films to guarantee solvency. But the public was confused and disappointed by *Little Giant* and *The Time of Their Lives,* and the two films failed to match the returns of the first ten A&C vehicles. Revenues continued to decline, and the committee management was swept out in a merger with the International Pictures Corporation headed by William Goetz and Leo Spitz. Uncle Carl Laemmle's company now had a new name, Universal-International. Spitz was a lawyer who had advanced to executive positions in the film industry without any discernible understanding of film making. Goetz had been in production at 20th Century-Fox, in which his father-in-law, Louis B. Mayer, had invested to get him the job. Chafing under the ego of Darryl F. Zanuck, Goetz left 20th Century-Fox to join with Spitz in International, which produced a number of pretentious but largely unsuccessful films.

An art collector with a distinguished collection, Goetz had no sympathy for the cheap westerns and tits-and-sand movies that had been the staple of the previous Universal regime—and why the American public patronized the low comedics of Abbott and Costello baffled him. Goetz announced that henceforth Universal-International would dispense with the potboiler westerns and costume dramas and would concentrate on films of importance and meaning. That policy would head Universal toward its second near-bankruptcy.

What to do with Bud and Lou? Goetz would have preferred to usher them to the studio gate, along with the horse wranglers, harem girls, and other relics of the previous regime. But it would have been imprudent to part with the two comedians who were still Universal's most important assets. Goetz received help from Robert Arthur, who had been lured to Universal from a contract at M-G-M as writer and associate producer of musicals. An urbane, college-educated man, Arthur nonetheless had a talent for combining nonsense with showmanship, and he was assigned to seek out a vehicle for Abbott and Costello.

Enough of pathos, Arthur declared. Bud and Lou needed

to return to their basic, lowdown, knockabout comedy. Their biggest hit had been *Buck Privates*. Arthur, himself recently returned from army service, reasoned that the next vehicle should be *Buck Privates Come Home*. He put together a script with Frederic Rinaldo and Robert Lees, combined it with routines from John Grant, cast expert farceurs such as Nat Pendleton, Don Porter, and Donald MacBride, and assigned the reliable Charlie Barton to direct. The mixture worked well, and Bud and Lou were totally cooperative, leaving their card game promptly when called for a scene.

Arthur suggested a departure for his second film with Bud and Lou. D. D. Beauchamp and William Bowers had written a screenplay, with James Stewart in mind as a western gunman forced to care for the widow and seven kids of a man he had shot. Strapped for money, the writers sold the script outright to Universal for $2,500. It lay dormant until producer Arthur decided it could be refashioned for Abbott and Costello. Goetz was dubious, but he said Arthur could produce *The Wistful Widow of Wagon Gap* if it could be made cheaply. Marjorie Main was borrowed from M-G-M to play the widow, and her style combined well with Lou's.

In its first year Universal-International released a number of prestigious films, including *A Double Life*, which won the Academy award for Ronald Colman as best actor, as well as *Odd Man Out, Black Narcissus, Great Expectations*, and other English films from J. Arthur Rank. The box office returns were negligible compared to the profits of *Buck Privates Come Home* and *The Wistful Widow of Wagon Gap*.

Listed in the credits for *The Wistful Widow of Wagon Gap* was the name of Sebastian Cristillo as associate producer. It was the ultimate in nepotism and sentiment; Lou had insisted that his father be hired as consultant on a western. Papa Cristillo adored westerns, and his New Jersey fantasies were realized when he and his wife moved to California. He met such heroes as Hoot Gibson and Ken Maynard. He became friends with Leo Carrillo, whom he visited on film locations; Papa showed up in his own western costume, including boots and six-shooter.

The Cristillos were happy in California. Mary became ac-

*The Little Flower and
friends* (above)

*Bud, Betty, and older brother
Harry Abbott, a favorite
of Lou's*

*Lou's brother Pat visits on
the set* (below)

tive in the Movie Stars' Mothers Club, and Sebastian enjoyed cooking huge, aromatic Italian meals for his family and friends. Lou urged them to fly back to Paterson whenever they were homesick, and they sometimes did. Sebastian kept a paternal eye on Lou's career, and he could admonish his son, as could no one else, when he believed that Lou had gone haywire. Eddie Sherman understood this, and in extremities he called upon the father to help control Lou. "You listen to this man," Sebastian told his son. "Eddie Sherman put bread on your table."

Sherman once recruited Papa Cristillo to help save the radio show. *The Abbott and Costello Program* was one of radio's successes, usually scoring in the top ten in the audience ratings. After the show had been on the air four years, Lou summoned Sherman and declared, "I want you to add a couple of writers to the radio staff."

"Gee, Lou, we don't have any budget for more writers," Sherman replied. "We can only hire four."

"Okay, fire two guys."

"Who do you want to hire?"

"My brother Pat and my brother-in-law Joe Kirk."

Sherman was shocked. "Pat and Joe don't know how to write comedy," he protested.

"I want them on the show," Lou said firmly. "That's an order."

The manager was forced to comply. He realized the show would suffer by the subtraction of two professional writers, so he devised a cover-up. He had heard of a young aspiring writer whose material seemed clever. Sherman hired the young man to submit three minutes of Abbott and Costello material each week for $100 and no credit. Sherman gave the material to Pat Costello for submission at the story meeting. Joe Kirk arrived with jokes he had picked up from friends. For their efforts they were paid $500 a week.

As Lou was reviewing the material at a script session, he came to a section that made him roar with laughter. "Who wrote this?" he asked.

"I did," said Pat.

"It's funny, real funny," said Lou. Afterward he told Eddie Sherman to raise Pat's salary to $750.

Sherman was incensed. He decided to cut off the flow from the $100-a-week closet writer and let Pat fend for himself. Predictably, the show dipped in quality and began losing listeners. Sherman believed it faced the danger of cancellation if the decline continued. He realized the need for stern measures, and so he went to see Papa Cristillo.

Sebastian poured his homemade wine and floated peaches in it, and the two men sat down to discuss the problem. Sherman explained the need for competent writers to stop the program's downhill slide. "You fire those-a two guys!" Sebastian exploded. "You musta protect my Louie. You fire Pat and Joe and get some-a good writers. You leave Louie to me. I take-a care of him."

After the next radio show, Sherman drew Pat Costello and Joe Kirk aside and told them they were being replaced by two new writers. Surprisingly, there was little protest. Lou raised no objection, his father having lectured him. The fresh writing talent picked up the show's quality, and the ratings started to rise. Then Sebastian Cristillo died. One morning in May 1947 he fell over dead. He had lived sixty-seven years.

Lou telephoned Eddie Sherman. In a cold voice that Eddie had never heard before, Lou told him, "I'm firing you."

"What?" Eddie said. "What for?"

"You killed my father."

"What the hell are you talking about?"

"You heard me. You killed my father. Joe said you did. You got Pop so upset about the ratings and Pat and Joe writing on the show that it killed him."

"Lou, this is crazy. I loved your father as much as you did. I only acted out of concern for you, and so did he."

"I gotta believe my family. You're fired."

"In the first place, you can't fire me. I got a contract for the next three-four years, so if you're looking for a lawsuit, you're gonna get it."

Lou remained firm. So did Eddie Sherman. He filed suit

138

The dedication ceremony for the Lou Costello Jr. Youth Foundation:
Lt. Gov. Goodwin Knight on the left and Gloria Jean
on the right (remember her?)

LOU COSTELLO JR.
YOUTH FOUNDATION
LOS ANGELES, CALIFORNIA

EARL HEITSCHMIDT AND CHARLES O. MATCHAM ARCHITECTS 417 SO. HILL ST. LOS ANGELES

to stop Universal's payments to Lou. Eddie and his wife went off to Europe, where he negotiated a contract for the rights to release a group of English-made movies on American television. When he returned, he discovered that Lou had been stricken with a recurrence of rheumatic fever and was unable to work. One day Eddie encountered Anne Costello in Beverly Hills. It was a joyful reunion.

"How's Lou?" Eddie asked.

"He's pretty sick," Anne said. "He talks about you a lot. I think he's sorry for what he did. I wish you'd give him a call."

"I'll do better than that. Tomorrow I'll drive out and see him."

"Would you really? I think that will make him better."

Eddie arrived at the Costello house the next day and went to Lou's bedroom. Lou's face brightened, and for two hours they talked as if nothing had interrupted their friendship. Finally Lou said, "I was a stupid fool to listen to Joe Kirk. I sure could use that money you've got tied up, and I bet you could use the commission. Do you want to drop it all?"

"Sure, Lou, why not?"

Lou sat up in bed, excited. "How much dough do you figure we got tied up?"

"I'd say four hundred thousand."

"That means forty thousand for your commission, right?"

"That's right, Lou."

"If I settle, will you give me ten thousand in cash?"

Always the angle. Lou would be getting $360,000 but he wanted to squeeze another $10,000 in cash. Eddie Sherman calculated the money he had received through Bud and Lou over the years, submerged his pride, and consented.

16

A Chapter about Bud

LET US SPEAK of Bud. There may be a tendency in this chronicle—has the reader detected it?—of allowing Lou to dominate. He tried to do it onstage, but Bud, with his ingrown, burlesque-wise sense of comedic proportion, would not allow him to. He always interjected his cautionary, "Now talk sense," and swung Lou back into balance. There were factors beyond Bud's control in movies—hence such excesses as *Little Giant* and *The Time of Their Lives*. And in business and career matters, Bud exerted little motivational force. That was not his style. Bud felt blessed by the fortune that had befallen him, and he hoped to prolong it as long as he could. Thus he was bewildered and disturbed by Lou's break with Eddie Sherman. During the schism Bud reported regularly to Eddie on the state of the team's fortunes and the whims of Lou's mind. Bud was delighted when Lou and Eddie reconciled and all three could once more function as a team.

Bud, though independent and freethinking, responded to Lou's moods. When Lou was happy, Bud was happy. When Lou was gloomy and suspicious of the studio, Bud was miserable. That meant trouble was in the offing. Bud's was a stolid personality. The key to his attitude was his salutation of "Hello, Neighbor." To Bud, who simply could not remember names, everyone was Neighbor. His old burlesque buddies were Neighbor, his directors were Neighbor, even Lou on occasion was Neighbor. Bud was thoroughly democratic about it; to him the president of Universal Pictures and the studio janitor were Neighbor. Radio writers became accustomed to being called by Bud "Neighbor" and by Lou, only slightly better at remembering names, "Tootsie." (This condition presented a problem when a young A&C writer, Leonard Stern, brought his mother to a broadcast. He finally introduced her to the stars as "Mrs. Tootsie.")

Bud possessed none of the fierce competitive drive that motivated Lou and brought him such grief. Bud was content to do his work and go home. The epilepsy had much to do with that. On a movie set his energies dwindled after four o'clock. If an attack came, Lou could usually stop it with the punch to the solar plexis. Sometimes Bud would start drinking beer, and then he was useless for filming. The assistant director, Joe Kenny, invented the expression, "Nothing's funny after five o'clock," and Bud often borrowed it when filming had stretched into the late afternoon. Directors learned to shoot Bud's important scenes earlier in the day, when his energies were still high.

The night brought terrors for Bud, and so he drank. He called for a drink, always Teacher's scotch with soda. The butler, Smallwood, prudently diminished the share of whiskey in each succeeding drink. Bud didn't require much. Three drinks, maybe four, and he would pass out blissfully. Later he would awake, have his dinner, then return to sleep. Always he awoke early, sans hangover, ready for the new day's work. He started breakfast with a tall glass of milk, then departed for the studio; usually he was the first to arrive on the set. Bud never drove a car, of course, because of the danger of his epilepsy.

Bud was proud of his estate at 4504 Woodley Avenue in the Valley. It had seventeen rooms to start with, and he added on, making room for the two children that he and Betty had adopted—Buddy, Jr., in 1944, and Rae Victoria in 1949. Bud was not an attentive father, though he tried; it was a role he simply couldn't manage. He himself had been reared in the

Lutheran church, and his children had the same upbringing. He was not a religious man; yet he did have a certain faith. When his wife Betty sprained her back and was paralyzed for a time, Bud read to her from the Bible. He surprised her with his knowledge of Scripture and his understanding of it. In 1950, when they had been married thirty-two years, Bud and Betty went through another ceremony in the Jewish faith. It was Betty's idea as a tribute to Bud's Jewish mother, whom Betty adored.

Lou's trademark was his cigar; Bud smoked a cigarette, always with a gold holder. Bud loved simple food and insisted on Betty's cooking even when they could afford a cook. He liked spareribs, sauerkraut, and beef stew and objected only to carrots and parsley. He hated to find parsley on his plate. He was a simple man, almost apolitical but leaning to the Democrats because of his family background; his uncle had been a power in Tammany Hall. Bud was a compliant man as well, and when Lou in later years insisted that they make appearances for Republican candidates and causes, Bud went along.

Bud never forgot nor denied his burlesque beginnings. To his way of thinking, burlesque people were the most enjoyable, the most reliable class of citizens. Word spread along what was left of the burlesque wheels that Bud Abbott was always good for a touch, and Bud's house and his café, the Backstage, became stopping places for burlesque performers when they reached the West Coast. Bud often ordered patrons of the Backstage out of the place—no charge for their unfinished dinners and half-consumed drinks. Then he and his companions from the Minsky years would drink and reminisce about old times.

Bud and Betty often entertained at home with elaborate catered affairs for four hundred people who gathered under a circus tent stretched over the Abbott acreage. Only once was the frivolity endangered. That came when Bud, after an excess of Teacher's, stilled the orchestra, grabbed the microphone, and announced, "All right, everybody off my property." No one took him seriously.

The guests at the Abbott parties were old burlesque buddies and Bud's co-workers in films and radio—producers, directors, and writers, as well as assistant directors, publicists, script clerks, and prop men. Both Bud and Lou made little incursion on Hollywood society. They were acquainted with Bob Hope, Red Skelton, Eddie Cantor, Jack Benny, and other comedians and sometimes appeared with them on each other's radio shows or at benefits, but they rarely mingled socially. Never would Bud or Lou be invited to the homes of Hollywood's social leaders—Louis B. Mayer, David O. Selznick, Samuel Goldwyn, William Goetz, Darryl Zanuck, et al. This bothered Lou, but Bud was totally unconcerned.

Bud loved the touch of money, the sheer, tactile feel of currency. He always carried a large roll of bills on his person, and it diminished as the day progressed, particularly when he was out in public and exposed to touches by oldtime acquaintances. A constant companion was Charlie Murray, who had managed the Gayety burlesque theater in New York, later operated a bail bond office in Van Nuys and a burlesque night club, the Zomba, in Studio City. He drove Bud everywhere and often carried Bud's roll of bills. When Bud walked into the bar of the Brown Derby Restaurant in Hollywood, old buddies down on their luck approached him. "Give the Neighbor fifty bucks," Bud said over and over again.

Betty pleaded with Bud not to carry so much money. He allowed Betty to have charge accounts at the fashionable stores, but he didn't like her to have cash herself. Once she had lost $90; he never forgot it. Bud himself had $1,300 stolen from a New York hotel room; still he carried large amounts of currency. Betty liked furs and Bud didn't, yet he bought her a full-length mink when they came to California—and seven sables and ermines later. She didn't like jewelry and he did, so he ladened her with a $30,000 star sapphire, a diamond ring once owned by Mae West, and an eight-and-a-half-carat diamond. Bud collected cut and uncut diamonds and carried them in a velvet pouch. To selected friends he would empty the pouch and reveal a glittering display of gems.

Bud enjoyed money of all kinds. He had cufflinks, tie clips, and money clips made out of gold coins and ordered a $1,500 watch with a twenty-dollar gold piece as a case. He collected

144

gold coins and currency, including a framed sheet of ten uncut $10 bills. He had a canceled $10,000 bill, an 1891 dollar bill with Martha Washington's portrait, and an 1896 five-dollar bill with Rubensesque nudes. A favorite stunt of Bud's was to slap an ancient $100 bill on a bar and wait for the bartender's reaction. Talking to a reporter about his money collection, Bud rhapsodized, "Love that stuff. Just love it."

More than anything else, Bud loved to gamble. For a good card game, he would even give up his nightly ritual of drinking himself into slumber. One night Milton Berle watched with fascination as Bud and Lou played for table stakes hour after hour, thousands of dollars moving from one side to the other. The telephone rang. "Who could be calling at this hour?" Bud complained. Berle answered the phone and told Bud and Lou the message: "It's the studio calling. It's eight in the morning and you're supposed to leave for work." Bud opened the drapes and was startled to see the daylight.

Both Bud and Lou were content to play cards with each other, but the addition of other players added zest to the match. Their steadiest, and luckiest, opponent turned out to be a colorful figure called Mike the Greek. His name was Michael Potson, and he operated Colisimo's, a cabaret in southside Chicago, which meant that he had close connections with the Mob. He was an amiable fellow who shared Bud and Lou's love of cards. They met when Bud and Lou visited Chicago on a tour in 1941. Potson quickly recognized a good thing after a few poker hands, and he often made trips to California to continue the game. The prospect of easy winnings became so alluring that he moved West, buying a house a short distance from Bud's.

Their continual losses did not deter Bud and Lou from the games with Potson. They invited him to the studio, and he became the third man in the between-the-scene card games. Mike the Greek became such a steady visitor to the set that the assistant director, Joe Kenny, began listing him on the call sheet. When Potson appeared at ten o'clock one morning, Charlie Barton, the director, delivered a mock bawling out, reminding that he was listed on the production sheet for a nine o'clock call.

A few years later, Mike the Greek's unorthodox ways of

acquiring income drew the attention of the federal government, and he was indicted in Chicago for evading $162,166.44 in income taxes. Bud and Lou were called to testify about the marathon poker games, and Lou admitted, "It's hard to say that I lost nine-tenths of the time, but I lost most of the time." Lou estimated his losses around $15,000, Bud between $20,000 and $25,000. The figures were conservative. Mike the Greek testified he had won only $9,000 to $10,000 from Bud and Lou. The judge was unbelieving and gave him two years.

No hard feelings. When Mike the Greek returned to California in failing health, Bud and Lou resumed the games at his house. They kept dealing almost to the end, Mike playing his hands from inside the oxygen tent.

17

A Chapter about Lou

LET US NOW praise Lou Costello. The Chaplin estimate—that Lou was the best clown since silent films—might have been close to the truth. Although the basis of the A&C comedy was the verbal routines of John Grant, Lou was also a superb pantomimist. Directors like Charles Barton, Eddie Sutherland, Charles Lamont, and Earl Kenton who had worked in silent films recognized Lou's facility and used it. He was fat but he had been an athlete, and that sometimes surprised people.

In *Here Come the Coeds,* Lou was required to masquerade as a girl basketball player. A renowned basketball star had been hired to stage the game, and he instructed Lou in a condescending manner. Lou played along, asking, "How do I hold the ball?" and "Can't I just carry the ball instead of bouncing it?" Lou stood at half-court and inquired, "Can I throw the ball from here?" The star player smiled indulgently, then stared unbelievingly as Lou tossed a perfect shot into the basket.

We are praising Lou Costello in this chapter because of the author's fear of presenting a one-sided portrait. The bad things that Lou did are more dramatic, the good things less so. He was intensely human, both in his faults and his virtues, and it would be unfair to let one side outweigh the other. Morrie Davis, who dealt with Lou over the years as business manager of Universal Studio, favored the analogy of the little girl with the little curl in the middle of her forehead. That was Lou. He could be horrid, but there were many times when he could be very, very good.

His generosity was prodigal. Christmas was more than a holiday to him; it was a festival of giving. The season often began in the summer, when Lou was in New York on business and devoted hours to picking out toys at F. A. O. Schwarz. From October, the Costello garage remained locked as the packages mounted in number. In early December, Lou put up the Christmas decorations at his house, aided by a crew of studio electricians. Every window of the twenty-two rooms was outlined by colored lights and each front window featured a moving display—waving Santa Clauses and revolving pine trees. Two heroic-size Santas appeared on the roof, one with sleigh and animated reindeer. From the chimney came a shower of soap bubbles. On the lawn was another Santa, bowing and shouting messages of Christmas cheer; he was surrounded by wrapped packages and a forest of paint-sprayed trees. A movie screen showed cartoons of Woody Woodpecker and other entertainments. Citizens from all over Los Angeles came to Sherman Oaks to see the Lou Costello Christmas. Lou himself stood in front of the house and tossed candies into the windows of the cars as they inched along. The display dazzled his neighbors, one of whom was a young country singer and comedian named George Gobel. He lighted a single bulb in front of his house with a sign: "Merry Christmas—See our display across the street."

The Costello family's own Christmas was ceremonious. Despite the enormous display to the outer world, Lou insisted that no signs of Christmas appear inside the house until the children went to bed. No tree, no packages, no toys already assembled. That meant a scramble late Christmas Eve. Lou himself insisted on trimming the tree. One year he had to work late at the radio show, and when he returned home he discovered that the tree had been decorated by the butler. Lou went upstairs to his room and cried.

Lou had another ritual at Christmas. Weeks before the holiday, he began collecting foodstuffs. He went to nearby grocery stores and said to the manager, "I'm going to spend a thousand dollars in your place; what kind of deal can we make?" He and the manager negotiated for the store's overstock. The goods were assembled on picnic tables at the Costello house, then packed into burlap bags. Lou assembled a list of families in need: studio workers who had been laid off, church parishioners down on their luck, burlesque buddies who couldn't find work. The bags were loaded into a station wagon and delivered on the day before Christmas. He wouldn't allow his brother Pat to make the deliveries, lest he be recognized. Usually Milton Bronson did the work, with instructions that under no circumstances was he to reveal the identity of the donor. Lou made other benefactions without publicity. When he read in the newspaper of a family struck by extreme hardship, he dispatched a check to pay for hospital bills or a house mortgage. He instructed Joe Glaston never to publicize such gestures or he would be fired.

Of all Lou's generosities, the most commendable was the Lou Costello, Jr., Youth Foundation. Both Bud and Lou worked hard to build and maintain the handsome recreation center for the kids of east Los Angeles, not only making extensive tours to raise money to build it but donating from their own funds to keep it operating. When Lou fell ill again and they were unable to make public appearances, the center was donated to the city of Los Angeles with the provision that it continue to bear the name of Lou Costello, Jr., and be used for recreational activities. Bud and Lou had poured $260,000 into the center and they sold it to the city for the amount of their encumberances, $97,500.

Lou had a great fondness for children. Whenever a child visited the movie set, he stopped production and sat down to talk, sometimes taking the visitor on a tour of the studio in a motorcycle sidecar. Lou was immensely pleased when Anne gave birth to their third daughter, Christine, in 1949. The new baby helped assuage the memory of the death of Butch, a sorrow that was ever-present. Lou had had a bracelet bearing the boy's name welded together around his wrist, and he wore it all his life.

Lou sometimes drank. He was not methodical in his drinking, as was Bud. Lou simply drank to get high.

"Gimme a drink," he said to whoever was near the bar.

"What would you like?"

"I don't care, just gimme a drink." Scotch, bourbon or gin, he swallowed it like a Coke.

"Gimme another drink," he said.

His companions could tell when Lou was drunk. He put his hat on backwards and acted silly. Like Bud, he was a nice drunk. Never nasty. Loud sometimes. There was the night of Desi Arnaz's opening at the Copacabana in New York. A few drinks brought out Lou's affection for Arnaz and he called from his table in the unmistakable Costello voice, "Hiya, Desi." As Arnaz was warming up to his "Babalu" number, the cry came again, "Hiya, Desi." Arnaz's voice rose in pitch, and so did Lou's. Two bouncers approached Lou's table. He sprang up and dodged through the nightclub until his pursuers wrestled him to the floor and hurried him out the back door.

A favorite drinking companion in New York was Jackie Gleason, then rising as a television star. Lou, who suffered severe hangovers, was recovering from one in his suite at the Sherry-Netherland when a call came from Gleason. "Louie, this is Jackie," said Gleason. "I gotta see ya. C'mon over." Lou tried to profess illness, but Gleason could not be dissuaded. Lou and Eddie Sherman took a taxi to the Park Central Hotel, where Gleason maintained his headquarters.

They found him seated in a thronelike chair, his head wrapped in a satin turban, with two attendants wielding large fans. "Louie, my boy, come sit beside me!" Gleason exclaimed. He placed a bottle between them and urged Lou to have a drink. Lou winced, said it was not the best of mornings. Gleason insisted. "Well, just a sip," Lou said. Within an hour they had drained the bottle. Waiters arrived with tureens of spaghetti, which both Lou and Gleason adored. After huge plates of spaghetti and more drinks, Gleason announced they were going to Toots Shor's restaurant.

They occupied a corner table and spent the afternoon with

jokes and stories. Lou began telling Gleason of a remarkable seer in California, a man known as the Wizard. "You can pick out a playing card and he'll tell you what it is, no matter how far away you are," said Lou.

"This I gotta try," said Gleason.

"For a hundred bucks?" said Lou.

"You're on!"

They called for a deck of cards. Gleason cut them and selected the Jack of Diamonds. Lou lifted a telephone and asked the operator for a number in California. He waited. "Hello, is the Wizard there? . . . Would you put him on, please? . . . Just a moment." He handed the receiver to Gleason who heard the words, "Jack of Diamonds," then the line went dead.

"That's fantastic!" said Gleason. "You can't do it again."

Lou did. And again. Ten times he called the Wizard and ten times Gleason was told the card he was holding. He pleaded with Lou to tell him how it was done. Simple. Bud and Lou often worked the game. Lou called Bud and asked for The Wizard. Bud immediately started saying, "Spades . . . hearts . . . diamonds . . ." Lou interrupted to say, "Would you put him on, please?" Bud began counting, "Ace . . . king . . . queen . . . jack . . ." and Lou interrupted when the right card was reached. "Oh, boy, am I gonna make a lot of money on this little stunt!" Gleason exclaimed.

When he was good, he was very, very good; and when he was bad, he was horrid.

The affair of Dean Martin illustrates the dual nature of Lou Costello. It began in Philadelphia in 1946, when Bud and Lou were appearing at the Earle Theater. After their final appearance each night, Bud went out to drink with old burlesque friends. Lou and Eddie Sherman visited the nightclubs that Eddie had known as a Philadelphia booker. One of them was the Walton Roof, operated by Jack Lynch. Lou and Eddie arrived for the final show, which featured a singer with handsome Italian looks marred only by a large, acquiline nose. Eddie found the young man's voice unimpressive but noted how he held the attention of the women in the audience. Jack Lynch confided to Eddie, "I notice you were watching that guy Martin. Eddie, you're an old friend and I want to give you a tip: steer clear of him. He's got thirty different managers and each has got a piece of him. And he drinks." Eddie relayed the information to Lou.

Sherman had returned to California when he was telephoned by his and Lou's New York lawyer, I. Robert Broder. "Lou had me go to Philadelphia yesterday to sign a contract for him to manage Dean Martin," said Broder. "I think Lou is going to want you to represent the guy. Now Lou wants to get Martin's nose fixed, and I've got to find a surgeon who can do the job."

The surgery was performed at a fee of $400, which Lou paid. Eddie Sherman refused to represent Martin and suggested having agents at M.C.A. seek jobs for him. After Martin had appeared in a few engagements, Broder called Lou to report that the singer had charged merchandise amounting to $2,000 to Lou. Lou soured on the idea of sponsoring a singer on the road to fame. "Get rid of him," Lou instructed the lawyer.

Dean Martin joined with Jerry Lewis in 1946, and they soon became the hottest team since Abbott and Costello. Lou seemed pleased with his former protégé's prosperity, and when Martin and Lewis opened at Ciro's in Hollywood, he reserved a front-row table for ten. At the end of the performance, Lewis hurried to the Costello table. Martin didn't even say hello.

Lou telephoned Eddie Sherman the following day. "I got out that contract I had with Dean Martin," Lou said. "It still has two years to run. I'm gonna sue the bastard for breach of contract."

"What are you talking about, Lou?" Eddie said. "I was with you when you told Broder to drop Martin."

"That don't matter. I still got a contract."

"Lou, I think you'd be making a mistake to sue him. It could only be construed as jealousy."

"I don't care. Nobody's gonna slough me off. If he had just come over and sat down at the table, okay. But now I'm gonna make him pay."

Lou filed his suit in New York and told Louella Parsons, "When I discovered Martin and signed him, he was unknown and he was earning fifty dollars a week. I even advanced him enough to have his nose bobbed. . . . He hasn't even bothered so much as to call me during the past five years."

Eddie Sherman continued urging Lou to drop the suit. Lou refused. He wanted $20,000 as balm for the snub at Ciro's. Martin's lawyer said the singer was broke. Sherman suggested borrowing the $20,000 from Hal Wallis, who had Martin and Lewis under contract for films. The $20,000 was paid.

"Now make yourself a big man and tear up the check," Eddie Sherman urged.

"Like hell I will," said Lou.

Lou bet the entire $20,000 on a horse that ran eighth. His winnings in the Dean Martin affair vanished, and so did his acrimony. A year later, a benefit for the Lou Costello, Jr., Youth Foundation was held at the Orpheum Theater in Los Angeles. Among the stars who appeared were Dean Martin and Jerry Lewis. Without a hint of bitterness, the two most famous of movie teams changed positions, and Dean Martin played straight man to Lou Costello while Bud Abbott performed "Who's on First?" with Jerry Lewis.

18

The Wars with Universal, Continued

"HOW COME every time we make a picture you paint the studio and charge it to our production?"

Lou's plaint to Universal-International executives expressed his frustration with the labyrinthine patterns of studio financing which caused profits to dissipate in a myriad of phantom charges. He argued—with sound logic—that the A&C pictures were financing the highbrow films of the new Universal-International regime. Lou observed bitterly that he and Bud had completed two comedies, while a Joan Bennett drama remained in production and still required a Paris location.

Spitz and Goetz were unhearing to Lou's demand for bigger budgets for the Abbott and Costello films. The studio bosses saw no purpose in it. Besides, Universal-International had lost $12 million during the first year of its policy of abandoning B pictures. Faced with another tight budget on his third A&C film, Robert Arthur decided to make use of the studio's assets: Frankenstein's monster, Dracula, and the Wolf Man. The plot: Dr. Frankenstein needs a new brain for his monster, who is becoming too smart. What better prospect for the transplant than Lou Costello!

"You don't think I'll do that crap, do you?" said Lou after he read the script of *Abbott and Costello Meet Frankenstein*. "My five-year-old daughter can write something better than that."

"I'll make a deal with you, Lou," Arthur suggested. "You do the picture and I'll pay you fifty thousand dollars cash for your share of the profits."

"Fifty G's right now?" said Lou, savoring the prospect.

"Right now," the producer replied. Lou was ready to accept, but the transaction was forestalled for tax reasons. The head of production, William Goetz, didn't even read the script. "I don't think those guys are funny," he explained to Arthur. "If I read the script, I might not think that *it* was funny, and anything that I say might harm your picture." He added, dubiously, "Good luck and God bless you."

The reliable Charlie Barton returned to direct. Bela Lugosi did Dracula, Glenn Strange was the monster, and Lon Chaney, Jr., played the Wolf Man. The Invisible Man was introduced at the end, with Vincent Price speaking the lines. Despite Lou's doubts, the gimmickry worked. Abbott and Costello continued their re-ascent to national favor. Lou reacted in character. He demanded $25,000 more per picture or he wouldn't report to the next one, *Mexican Hayride*.

Universal-International suspended Bud and Lou. Bud didn't mind. Ordinarily he voiced no opinion of the scripts, either in movies or radio; he did his lines, collected the money, and went home. This time he declared that the *Mexican Hayride* script stank. Lou disagreed; he was enamored with the prospect of playing a comic bullfighter. With the distribution office clamoring for more Abbott and Costello films, Universal-International acquiesced to Lou's demands, and *Mexican Hayride* went into production. As it turned out, Bud was right.

Lou's work habits did not improve with the resurgence of his movie career. The dressing-room card games grew longer, causing consternation to assistant directors who were new to A&C films. When Bud was losing, he said, "Be there in a minute, Neighbor." When Lou was losing, he said, "Get lost." A veteran assistant director like Joe Kenny could say, with gruff good humor, "All right, get your ass in there; we got work to do," and Bud and Lou grumblingly reported to the set.

Howard Christie was another good match for Bud and Lou. He was a tough, burly football player from the University of

California, and he was dedicated to his job as assistant director. When Lou refused to leave a card game one day, Christie lifted him out of the chair and carried him to the camera. Lou thought it was funny. Afterward Christie and another assistant sometimes resorted to the ritual of carrying Lou in his chair from dressing room to set.

Contributing to the chaos of the Abbott and Costello sets was a round, bald tragicomic character named Bobby Barber. He had once possessed ambitions as a serious actor, but his small physique and plain looks limited him to bit parts in comedies of the 1930s. Then he met Bud and Lou. Bobby started with a tiny role as a waiter in *Hold That Ghost,* and he proved such an amusing foil off-camera that Bud and Lou insisted on hiring him for the duration of every picture. Sometimes he played a bellboy or a cabbie, sometimes not. Always he was the set's tummeler, stirring up excitement, generally as the butt of pranks. Bud and Lou gave him the hotfoot so many times that he took to wearing tennis shoes. They squirted seltzer in his pants, poured ketchup in his pockets, cracked eggs on his shiny pate. Bobby reacted histrionically to all the torment. When he was goosed, he leaped into the air like Nijinsky. Doused with a bucketful of water, he imitated a drowned seal.

When Charlie Barton finished a scene with Bud and Lou, he heard the noise of sawing behind the set. "Who the hell is making that noise?" the director demanded. He found Bobby Barton sawing wood. "I heard you say 'Cut!'" Bobby explained. In another scene Lou was being threatened with the third degree by a policeman. "Put down that hose, put down that hose!" Lou cried. Bobby dropped a fifty-foot garden hose from the overhead catwalk.

Bobby was in charge of the pies. Every morning he picked up a dozen or two from an Encino baker, who bragged to all his customers that Mr. Lou Costello, the comedian, was immensely fond of his pies. The pies were not for eating. Each day they found their way to the faces of the A&C entourage and others on the movie set. One day Lou smacked Bobby with a lemon meringue in the studio commissary, appalling Messrs.

Goetz and Spitz. Following a scene, Lou detained Charlie Barton under the lights to engage him in conversation. Charlie, whose career dated back to Mack Sennett, suddenly changed positions with Lou, who was bombed by a pie from above. "Goddammit, I had Bobby up there for two days trying to get you!" Lou cried.

Charlie Barton was a fun-loving man, but he also remained convinced that the director had to maintain charge of the movie set. Such an attitude inevitably brought clashes with Lou. Realizing that the A&C routines could not be repeated in films without boring the audience, Barton asked John Grant to write a new version of Packing-Unpacking. This was a scene in which Lou loaded and unloaded a valise as Bud repeatedly changed his mind about whether they should make an escape.

Bud and Lou started the routine before the camera one morning and Barton called, "Cut!"

"What's the matter?" Lou demanded. "Why do you break in when we're just gettin' started?"

"Because you're not doing the script," Barton replied. "John Grant wrote a new version. Didn't you read it?"

"Yeah, I read it and I don't like it," Lou said. "Bud and I are gonna do it the same way we've always done it."

"That's the trouble—you've done it too many times. We've got to get a new approach to it."

"Look, Charlie, I've been doing Packing-Unpacking for twenty years and it's never failed. We're gonna do it our way, and that's final. Period."

Barton shrugged and ordered a second camera to film the routine. He positioned himself under the camera nearest Bud and Lou and called, "Action!" Lou began the act of taking their belongings out of a dresser and stuffing them into a suitcase as Bud planned the getaway. Back and forth went the clothing as Bud switched signals. Barton sat straight-faced under the camera as Bud and Lou repeated the action. Finally Lou said to the director, "Why don't you say 'Cut!' or something?"

"I'm waiting for the funny stuff," Barton replied.

Lou exploded, "That's it—we're leaving. Come on, Bud,

we don't have to take this crap." Bud dutifully followed him off the stage. They remained away from the studio for two days, then returned and played the scene as written.

Charles Lamont was another comedy craftsman whose calm manner concealed a firm will. He directed a scene in which Lou bumped into an ambulance door. Next Lou bumped into the door of the hospital. Lamont halted the scene and asked, "What did you do that for?"

"I think it's funny," Lou replied.

"Once it's funny, twice it isn't," the director said.

"I think it's funny, and I'm gonna do it."

"Go ahead and knock your brains out. Don't forget: I'm the one who cuts the picture." Only one bump remained in the film.

Assistant directors like Joe Kenny and Red Christie could sense the onset of trouble on an A&C set, and they sidled to the telephone and called Robert Arthur. The producer hurried to the stage and used his diplomacy and reason to calm the situation. Joe Kenny called Arthur one day when *Mexican Hayride* was on location at Calabasas, at the eastern end of the San Fernando Valley. "Can you come right away?" the assistant director asked, giving no reason for the urgency. "Sure," said Arthur.

When he arrived at the hillside location, he could feel the tenseness in the company. Lou was in a bad humor. The studio had provided him with a telephone-equipped limousine so he could call his bookie. But the telephone would not function where the film was shooting. Whenever Lou wanted to lay a bet, he had to climb into the limousine and drive to the top of a nearby hill.

Bud was in a better mood. He had ordered cracked crab flown from the East Coast, and he invited Lou and Arthur to join him at lunch. As they savored the crab, Bud complained that a woman had telephoned the night before and talked on and on about using Bud's estate for a charity affair. After he finished his complaint, Lou giggled and admitted, "Yeah, she called me first, and I couldn't get her off the phone so I gave her your number."

"You gave her my number!" Bud exploded, and they argued back and forth during the rest of the lunch hour. As soon as Arthur returned to his office at the studio, there was another call from Joe Kenny. Lou had thrown a tantrum and left the location. The producer returned to the set and discovered that Charlie Barton could shoot no more without Lou. Now Bud erupted in a fit of loyalty, declaring, "If Lou goes, I go," and he went.

Arthur drove to Bud's house and asked, "If I can get Lou to come back, will you?" Bud said he would. Arthur proceeded to Lou's house and reported that Bud had walked off the set but would return if Lou would. Yes, he would, Lou replied, if the studio would agree to his demand for the 16mm rights to the A&C movies. The producer called the studio and approval was granted. Shooting resumed at Calabasas at 3:30 in the afternoon.

Lou realized that he and Bud had to present a united front to win their demands. Thus, whenever he planned a power play, he resolved his differences with Bud. Bud was always submissive, despite the indignities that Lou had subjected him to. And, despite his disproportionate share of their film earnings, Bud maintained an unswerving loyalty to his little partner and to the team.

One evening Robert Arthur was surprised when his wife Goldie told him that Bud Abbott was on the telephone. "But Bud has passed out by now," Arthur remarked. Bud's voice was unmistakable on the other end of the wire, and he seemed totally competent. In regard to Lou's latest demand for more money from the studio, Bud declared, "I've got to think of my little buddy. We've been together a long time, and whether he's right or wrong, I've got to stick by him. I support him one hundred percent in this fight. So tomorrow morning I want one million dollars in small bills at the studio gate. Otherwise I'm not coming to work. And that's final. Good night, Neighbor."

Bud reported to work at nine o'clock the next morning, remembering nothing of the conversation.

A major break between U-I and A&C had its beginnings in a stroll by Eddie Sherman along Vine Street as he left the NBC radio studios. He passed a Castle Films store that advertised: ABBOTT AND COSTELLO IN "OYSTERS AND MUSCLES." The manager told Sherman that he was selling 16mm shorts of Abbott and Costello routines from their Universal movies.

Sherman called Edward Muhl, business manager of Universal-International, and reminded him that the A&C contract forbade any use of portions of their films; Sherman had included the clause to preserve the team and prevent use of clips without Bud. Muhl was evasive, as were other company executives. And so William A. Abbott and Louis Cristillo filed a suit against Universal Pictures asking $5 million in damages for misuse of their films as well as failure to share profits in re-releases of the features. While in England, Sherman had learned that reissues of the A&C movies were doing better business than the original runs. Also, Universal had vindictively brought back old A&C releases to compete with their first independent film, *The Noose Hangs High*. Payments to Bud and Lou hadn't reflected the added income, since no one had foreseen the huge income from reissues.

The suit permitted Abbott and Costello to peruse the company's accounting books, and they proved good reading. The many items charged to the A&C films included a penthouse in Manhattan for one of the Universal executives. After Bud and Lou had given their depositions in New York, Nate Blumberg, the Universal president, sought a conference with Eddie Sherman. "This is getting ugly," said Blumberg. "I'd like to talk it out and come to some understanding."

Sherman was willing. He started his demands for a settlement: fifty percent of the profits on the shorts in distribution, and no more to be issued. Okay, said Blumberg. Sherman wanted accounting on the reissued features with Bud and Lou's percentages being reinstated in perpetuity. That's tough, said Blumberg. Then the suit continues, said Sherman. Give me time, said Blumberg.

Rather than expose the corporation laundry in public, Blumberg acquiesced. But dignity had to be maintained, and he exacted a promise that details of the settlement would not be disclosed. The suit was dismissed, and Bud and Lou issued a statement expressing "regret over any injury that might have been caused Universal by various charges made during the suit." Bud and Lou didn't mind observing the formalities. They had realized $2 million because of Eddie Sherman's stroll down Vine Street.

19

Where Did All the Dollars Go?

"DON'T FORGET, fellas, you're partners with Uncle Sam."

Eddie Sherman kept reminding Bud and Lou to honor their income tax obligations, but they chose not to listen. After all, the flow of money was unceasing; taxes would somehow be paid. Both Bud and Lou had financial advisors, and all were bad. Bud, the archetypal con man on the screen, allowed himself to be gulled into one hapless investment after another. When he was urged to place his earnings in certain winners, such as California land, he recoiled like a man who was threatened with a swindle.

Lou, who was making more money, managed to get rid of more. He continued improving the Longridge property, circling the acreage with a miniature steam train and stocking a pond with trout. He started a racing stable and soon had twenty-three horses. Not plain American horses; he bought his in Ireland. In 1946, he and Bud had earned more salary than anyone else in the United States—$469,170.60, and their income continued growing. Yet Lou repeatedly uttered pleas of poverty.

"Bob, I can't even pay my milk bill," Lou complained to producer Arthur. "I'm up to my ass in debt. Can't you go to the bosses and get me an advance?"

The sympathetic Arthur agreed to try. He described Lou's

plight to Leo Spitz, whose compassion for Abbott and Costello was nil. But he feared that a disgruntled Lou would sabotage the film in progress, and so he authorized a $100,000 check. He handed it to Arthur and said, "You've got to deal with him; you give it to him."

Arthur strode down to the A&C stage and told Lou, "I've got a present for you."

Lou accepted the $100,000 check without a word, walked to the telephone and dialed. "I'll take that yacht," he said.

Lou's investments almost matched Bud's in their unworthiness. One was an oil-drilling venture in Montana. Morrie Davis asked Lou how it was progressing. "Great!" Lou replied. "We went through oil and sand and hit an underground lake. If I could just move that lake to Los Angeles, I'd make a fortune."

Lou's betting was prodigious. Robert Arthur observed him at Santa Anita, where a Costello horse, Lolly C., was running. Lou wagered $5,000 in win tickets at the parimutuel windows. So he would not force down the odds, he placed an additional $12,000 with a bookie. Lolly C. finished last.

Alex Gottlieb once asked Lou what had been his largest bet. Lou recalled a visit to Florida's Gulfstream Track, then notorious for its fixed races. He encountered a gambler friend who counseled him to bet $50,000 on a horse in the eighth race. Lou was reluctant to bet such an amount, but the friend assured him, "If that horse doesn't win, there'll be a lot of dead jockeys around here." Lou followed the advice and bet the $50,000.

After a few furlongs, Lou's horse was well in front, the opposing jockeys straining hard to keep their mounts behind. The smiling Lou turned to his brother Pat and remarked, "The only way my horse can lose is if it stumbles and falls down." It did.

Workers on A&C movie sets learned to gauge Lou's gambling success or failure by his attitude each morning. If he arrived on the stage with a cheery smile, he had fared well the night before. Often he bragged, "I won twenty thousand bucks last night." When he appeared glum and irritable, it was sure evidence that the cards had been against him.

Lou's reputation as a loser won him admittance into the biggest game in town. It was a circle that included Hollywood's toughest gamblers, high-powered men who waged millions in movie deals and liked to play cards for high stakes. They included Joe Schenck, Mike Todd, Eddie Mannix, Bert Friedlob, and, occasionally, Sid Grauman and Irving Berlin. They welcomed the amusing little comic, Lou Costello, who had a zest for poker and an unfailing penchant for losing.

One day Milt Bronson, Lou's driver and companion, stopped by Eddie Sherman's office. He was carrying a shoe box, and Eddie asked what was in it. Bronson opened the box and disclosed stacks of new currency. "It's what Lou lost last night —ninety thousand dollars," Bronson said. "I've got to deliver it to Eddie Mannix at M-G-M; he's the banker who settles all the winnings and losings the next day." Despite his losses, Lou continued playing. He enjoyed being invited to wager with such important figures.

Bud and Lou found another place to dispose of their money: Las Vegas.

It started in 1947 when Eddie Sherman was telephoned by George Raft. "Can you come up to my house?" the actor asked. "I want you to meet a friend of mine." Sherman drove to Raft's home on Coldwater Canyon and was introduced to "Mr. Siegel," a handsomely dressed man with dark good looks and an undeniable air of authority.

"Mr. Siegel owns the Flamingo Hotel in Las Vegas," Raft explained to Eddie. "Eddie is not only Abbott and Costello's manager, he's their boss," Raft told Siegel.

"I'd like Bud and Lou to play the Flamingo," said Siegel.

"That's nice," said Sherman, unimpressed. His agent's mind calculated the $5,000 to $6,000 weekly fees that name acts had been paid by El Rancho Vegas and the Last Frontier in Las Vegas.

"How much do you want for the boys?" Siegel inquired.

"Twenty-five thousand a week," Sherman replied.

Siegel's face remained expressionless. "When are they available?" he asked.

Sherman told him.

"I'd like them for two weeks," said Siegel.

Sherman remained unpersuaded. "I'll need to have the money in advance."

"Would tomorrow morning be all right? Say eleven o'clock?"

"That would be fine."

When Sherman returned to his office, George Raft was on the phone. "Jesus, Eddie, you sure were tough," said Raft. "Money in advance?"

"Hell, yes. I can't let the boys play a date and not get paid. Your Mr. Siegel talks big, but I don't know who he is."

"You don't know who he is? Ben Siegel?"

"No."

"*Bugsy* Siegel?"

"Is that supposed to mean something?"

"All I can say, Eddie, is, don't cross him."

Sherman returned to Raft's house the next morning with the signatures of Bud and Lou on a contract. Siegel tossed him a brown envelope. "Here's the money—count it," he said. Sherman opened the package and counted the stacks of new currency. He removed his commission and delivered the rest to Bud and Lou. They arrived at the Flamingo the day prior to the beginning of the engagement. Before they went onstage opening night they had lost their entire salaries at the gambling tables. By the end of the two weeks they had lost another $50,000.

Other casino operators quickly learned of the Abbott and Costello bonanza. Next Bud and Lou worked for Beldon Katleman at El Rancho Vegas. On the night before the opening, Katleman invited Eddie Sherman to dine with him and attend the closing show, which starred Joe E. Lewis. During the congenial evening, Sherman noticed that an assistant periodically arrived and whispered to Katleman, who nodded. At the end of the show, the assistant appeared again.

"How far do you want Bud to go?" Katleman asked Sherman.

"What do you mean?" Sherman replied.

"How much credit do you want me to extend him? Right now he's thirty-five thousand in the hole."

"You stop him right now!" Sherman exploded.

Sherman found Bud standing unhappily at the crap table. "They said I can't have any more credit, Eddie," he complained.

"You're damn right," said Eddie. "Don't you realize that you've already blown more than your earnings on the whole engagement?"

"That's all right, Neighbor. I'll get it back." Bud tried his luck at other casinos, with predictable results.

Eddie would not book Bud and Lou into Las Vegas for years afterward. But Bud managed to return on his own. After a visit to the Desert Inn, he and Betty boarded the 6 A.M. flight back to Los Angeles. She gazed around the airplane and commented, "Isn't that nice?"

"Isn't what nice?" Bud asked.

"One of the men from the hotel is on the plane to see us home."

"Yeah," said Bud, "he's coming back to collect the sixty-five grand I dropped at the tables."

Such losses didn't discourage Bud for long. He kept trying to beat the cards and dice, and sometimes he succeeded. After one lengthy poker game, Betty carried home $20,000 in her brassiere. Usually he lost, but what did it matter? The money kept rolling in.

And then one day an agent from the Internal Revenue Service came knocking at Bud's door.

20

Television and the
Winds of Change

THE 1950s brought years of transition. The War in Korea ended the hope that America's youth would no longer die in battle. The Cold War unleashed the Nixon-McCarthy demagogues in search of lives to ruin. After two tumultuous decades, Americans found solace in the stolid paternalism of Dwight Eisenhower.

Change came fast in the entertainment world. Television brought a revolution more sweeping than sound motion pictures. New stars emerged, old stars found fresh popularity as Americans embraced the new medium. The movie studios reacted with the same head-in-sand attitude that greeted talkies in 1928. Television would never destroy the American habit of going out to the movies, the moguls said, while neighborhood theaters closed by the hundreds.

Television was a natural for Bud Abbott and Lou Costello. Their burlesque routines, minicomedies in themselves, were ideally suited to the limited attention span of television viewers. Their comedy was elemental, it appealed to all ages and all shades of sophistication, it bordered on the violent—vital factors for television appeal.

By 1950 the coaxial cable had made its way across the continent, permitting coast-to-coast telecasts. The first of the bigtime shows to emanate from Hollywood was *The Colgate*

167

Comedy Hour, on which star comics sold toothpaste and soap chips. Each week brought a different star or comedy team—Bob Hope, Eddie Cantor, Donald O'Connor, Jimmy Durante, Jack Carson, Abbott and Costello, Martin and Lewis.

Bud and Lou were clearing $15,000 for *The Colgate Comedy Hours,* but that wasn't enough for Lou. He told Eddie Sherman: "I wanna do a series of TV shows—fifty-two of 'em. We'll get some kind of a story line and we'll weave all of our routines into it. That way we'll own the routines, you understand? You get somebody to put the money up, and Bud and I will work for free. Then we'll sell the series to a network and make a bundle. You find the money, little man. I know you can do it."

The timing was right. Ratings for the Abbott and Costello shows on *The Colgate Comedy Hour* had been excellent, and NBC was eager for a second year's contract. Sherman had calculated that the series Lou proposed could be produced for $15,000 per episode, not including salaries for Bud and Lou. Sherman proposed to Sylvester (Pat) Weaver, president of NBC, that the network finance the filming of twenty-six shows with an option to buy them; Bud and Lou would then appear in a second session of eight *Colgate Comedy Hours.* Weaver agreed.

Alex Gottlieb, who had produced seven A&C movies at Universal, was enlisted as producer, and he devised a format that integrated the routines. Jean Yarbrough, who had directed three of the Universal films, was assigned to direct. The customary cast included Sid Fields, an old burlesque hand who helped prepare the scripts, Hillary Brooke, Gordon Jones, and Joe Besser, plus the old A&C regulars, Joe Kirk, Bobby Barber, Milton Bronson, and a chimpanzee named Bingo.

NBC's reaction to the first three episodes was favorable, and the network offered the series to advertisers. Admiral Television made a proposal to buy *The Abbott and Costello Show* for $40,000 per episode and present it on NBC at eight o'clock Monday night. Both Eddie Sherman and Alex Gottlieb urged Lou to accept.

168

"No," Lou replied. "It's not enough money. I want sixty grand for the show."

"Lou, they just aren't paying that much for a half-hour comedy," Sherman argued.

"They will for this one. I want sixty grand. And I don't want to be on Monday night."

"Why not?" Gottlieb asked.

"Because when I was in burlesque, Monday night was always the worst night of the week. Same way with legit, same way with movies. You play to empty houses on Monday."

"But that was in *theaters*, Lou," the producer argued. "This is television. The average family goes out and spends money on the weekend, then they have to stay home on Monday night. It's a great night for television."

"I don't think so," Lou said flatly.

Sherman reluctantly informed NBC that the Admiral proposal was not acceptable. Filming proceeded on the first twenty-six shows. After ten episodes had been completed, Lou told Gottlieb, "We don't need you anymore. We know how to make these shows now."

"Okay, Lou," said the producer. "You can fire me, but it's going to cost you a lot of money. I have a firm contract to make twenty-six shows, with an option for twenty-six more."

"I'll pay you off," Lou said. "I want my brother Pat to be the producer."

With Pat Costello as the nominal producer, the twenty-six shows were completed. NBC offered them to other sponsors, and there were no takers. Lou was getting anxious. Not only did he have twenty-six half-hours that the network couldn't sell; he had also produced a twenty-six-part series *I Am the Law* starring George Raft, and it remained unsold.

MCA, the giant talent agency, had recently entered the field of television production and distribution, and its president, Lew Wasserman, asked for rights to distribute the two series. He proposed selling them in individual cities, with a syndication fee of forty percent of the gross receipts. The terms were stiff, but Lou agreed. Chevrolet bought sponsorship of *The Abbott and Costello Show*, and it was scheduled on CBS stations Friday nights, starting December 5, 1952. Lou got the night of the week he wanted, but not the hour. *The Abbott and Costello Show* played at 10:30, following the regular network programing and after the juvenile fans of Bud and Lou had been sent to bed.

NBC sought a third season of Bud and Lou on the *Colgate Comedy Hour*, and again Eddie Sherman won a concession. NBC would guarantee a four percent loan from Bankers Trust in New York for financing of the second twenty-six episodes of *The Abbott and Costello Show*. Bud had been wary of the whole enterprise, and he declined to defer his salary, insisting on $7,500 per show. Lou paid him for the first twenty-six shows, then the checks came more slowly and finally stopped. Bud demanded his money, Lou stalled. Bud threatened to sue, Lou said, "Go ahead."

Eddie Sherman was deeply concerned. If Bud sued Lou over the payment, the publicity would be extremely damaging to the team. As far as the public knew, Abbott and Costello had worked in harmony since the schism of 1945. Sherman persuaded Bud and Lou to attend a conference with their attorneys to seek an agreement. After much name-calling between Bud and Lou, a deal was made: In lieu of his salary for the rest of the shows, Bud would receive twenty-five percent of all receipts from the series.

The television appearances brought Bud and Lou renewed popularity, emboldening Lou to new disputes with Universal-International. Despite the A&C contributions to corporative health, Goetz and Spitz still considered them low comics who deserved nothing more than B-picture budgets. Most of the studio's important films were now being photographed in color; all of the Abbott and Costello movies for Universal were in black and white. If Bud and Lou wanted quality, they would have to go elsewhere.

Warner Brothers was eager to make films with Abbott and Costello, especially under the terms that Eddie Sherman offered. He had acquired financing from Bankers Trust, which had

Mack Sennett, more or less at the wheel (above)

Charles Laughton does a double take (left)

Giving DiMaggio the business

provided the backing for the second season of *The Abbott and Costello Show*. First Lou's company would produce a film, then Bud's. Each carried a budget of $450,000. Bud would be paid $200,000 to appear in Lou's film, and Lou's company would keep the profits. Lou would perform in Bud's film under the same conditions.

Both Bud and Lou wanted Alex Gottlieb to produce their films. Even though he had been summarily dropped from the television series, Gottlieb agreed to return. "I'll produce the pictures on one condition," he told Eddie Sherman.

"What's that?" the agent asked.

"That I don't have to play cards with Bud and Lou."

"That will be no problem. They both want to make their pictures as inexpensively as possible."

Lou's movie came first. Ever conscious of his kid audience, he decided to make a fairy tale, *Jack and the Beanstalk*. It was the first A&C film in color, and Gottlieb gave it as much production value as was possible on the limited budget. Jean Yarbrough directed, and there were no delaying poker games, no four o'clock finishes. Lou kept things moving.

Bud's picture was *Abbott and Costello Meet Captain Kidd*. A strong actor was needed for the pirate, and Gottlieb suggested Charles Laughton. But would the distinguished actor submit to such buffoonery? Surprisingly, he was interested. Gottlieb took the script to Boston, where Laughton was appearing in a play. "I'll do it," said the actor. Before returning to California, Gottlieb could not resist asking Laughton why. "Because I never have been able to do a double take," he explained. "If I do a picture with Lou Costello, I can learn."

Both films were money makers; in fact, the Bankers Trust complained that its loans were repaid too quickly. *Jack and the Beanstalk* was less successful, partly because Lou, at forty-six, seemed unconvincing as the youthful giant killer. *Captain Kidd* had more adult appeal and drew greater profits—a fact which Bud enjoyed repeating to Lou.

21

Troubles

"HOW MUCH do you pay for your suits, Mr. Abbott?" the Internal Revenue Service auditor asked.

"Two hundred and seventy-five dollars," Bud replied.

"Isn't that a lot of money for a suit?"

"I dunno. Is it?"

"I pay seventy-five dollars for my suits."

"Yeah, but you aren't starring in movies. You don't have to look that good."

"You wear those suits when you're not in motion pictures, don't you?"

"Sure, I wear them on television, personal appearances—"

"I mean you also wear them when you're not performing."

"Sometimes."

"One hundred and fifty dollars is all the government can allow as a business expense. Now this item of the shoes. Twenty-nine dollars for a pair of shoes?"

"That's unusual?"

"It is to me. I can get a pair for——"

"I know, I know. *You* can buy 'em cheaper. But don't you understand that a straight man can't look like everybody else. I've always paid a lot of money for my clothes, even when I was in burlesque. That's part of the trade."

"Twenty-nine dollars is more than we can allow for a pair of shoes. . . ."

And so it went, Bud answering the questions for a change.

Bud—angry, confused, frustrated, disillusioned, and, in the end, defeated. He had taken much of his salary in cash and blown it at the tables in Las Vegas, over cards with Mike the Greek, in handouts to burlesque buddies, on drinks for everybody at the Backstage. His accountants, who were incompetent and unconcerned, didn't help. The government moved with bureaucratic overkill, sifting through all of Bud's records from 1947 to 1953. The decision: Bud owed a half-million dollars in disallowed deductions. And the penalties started from the first miscalculated pair of shoes.

Having nabbed the straight man, the bureaucrats next pursued the comic.

Lou was equally vulnerable, perhaps more so, since his accountant was not only incompetent but crooked. Besides juggling accounts, the accountant had neglected to pay $200,000 in payroll taxes for Lou's corporation. Lou was ready to send him to jail, but his heart was softened by pleas from the accountant's wife. The man moved on to San Francisco, resumed the same tactics, and landed in jail.

Lou hired a new accountant, Ralph Handley, to clean the Augean stables of his finances. Lou had a policy of never allowing anyone full rein over his affairs; Handley insisted on complete charge. He fired incompetents and hired new help. The government found that Lou had omitted some of his Las Vegas income from his tax returns and had written off his yacht as a business expense. Although the money from personal appearances went directly to the Lou Costello, Jr., Youth Foundation, the I.R.S. insisted that the earnings had to be reported as income. When the agents were finished, they calculated that Lou owed the government $750,000.

In 1953 Lou talked openly about his finances in an interview. Eddie Sherman was present, and he confirmed that for several years Bud and Lou had been earning a total of $1,750,000 annually from all sources—movie salaries, movie percentages, radio, television, theater appearances. Yet they had been able to save nothing.

"I'm not complaining about paying taxes," Lou told me.

174

"I realize that we have to keep taxes high to pay for the fight against communism. But I want to show what some high earners are up against. I have to estimate how much money I'm going to get in the coming year and keep paying taxes while the money is coming in. I've already paid forty thousand dollars this year and I'm fifty thousand behind. If I fail to estimate correctly for any quarter, I get penalized."

Sherman calculated that a million dollars a year came from movies, the rest from other areas of entertainment. Then he cited the outgo: $100,000 for writers, $175,000 in agent's commissions; $40,000 legal fees; $75,000 accounting fees; $30,000 travel; $50,000 entertainment; $10,000 clothes; large contributions to charity and to the friends and relatives who expected to be supported by Bud and Lou. Sherman said that the boys (everyone still called them "the boys," although Bud was nearing sixty) were in the 94-percent tax bracket. Bud, who joined the interview following a movie-set conference with Internal Revenue agents, added that he was in a 110-percent bracket because of penalties on back taxes.

"I haven't been able to save a dime," said Lou. "I can't afford to quit working, and I certainly can't afford to die. The taxes would wipe out my family."

They might as well have been reciting "Who's on First?" or the Mustard Routine, for all the sympathy they received, either from the I.R.S. or the general public. Who cared about the tangled finances of a couple of comics? Who indeed? Not even Bud and Lou seemed to care. Lou continued to race his stable of thoroughbreds and to bet crazily. One day he told Eddie Sherman: "I gotta have fifty thousand dollars, tomorrow at the latest; I gotta fly to Detroit with it. If I don't, I'm dead. Get it for me, little man." Sherman went to executives a NBC, where Abbott and Costello were an important part of the *Colgate Comedy Hour*. The executives agreed to a $50,000 advance on Lou's salary. Sherman delivered the cash to Lou, who flew off to Detroit to satisfy his creditors.

For a while, at least, Bud was able to stand off the I.R.S. men. They forced the sale of Bud's five expensive automobiles.

The following day he went to the showroom and bought a brand-new Cadillac. "I gotta have some way of getting to work," he reasoned.

The money problems were exacerbated by Lou's illnesses, long months when Bud and Lou were unable to generate any new income. During the years from 1943 to 1953, Lou suffered three serious attacks of rheumatic fever, an operation for removal of a gangrenous gall bladder, a near-drowning internally because of excess fluid in tissues. Each time Bud reacted with sympathy and concern for his "little buddy," in spite of the disputes they had known. Bud was on his yacht with Charlie Barton at Catalina Island when a message came about Lou's gall bladder operation. "I've got to see Lou," Bud said, and he chartered an airplane to return him to the mainland.

The closest time for Bud and Lou came during the European tour of 1953. Val Parnell, impresario of the London Palladium, had been seeking an engagement by Bud and Lou for years, but their schedule didn't allow it. Finally it was arranged. Bud and Lou went in style, of course. Suites aboard the *U.S. United States* for Bud, the *Queen Mary* for Lou. Bud took along Betty and his niece Betty, as well as Tommy Amato, his bodyguard. Lou had Anne and the three daughters, a nurse for the youngest, Lou's mother and aunt, his doctor and his wife and child. When Bud and Lou arrived in London, the press reaction was overwhelming. Abbott and Costello had been great favorites with the English throughout the war and afterward.

Bud and Lou first played a date in Scotland, then the families parted for touring. They were spending movie receipts that had been prohibited from export from countries hard-pressed by the postwar economy. Lou complained that the Universal representatives didn't give him enough, and he telephoned his protests to the studio. Bud had no such problem when he arrived in Rome. The Universal representative came to the Hotel Excelsior with a suitcase stuffed with *lire*.

In London, both parties stayed at the Savoy Hotel, and Lou and Anne joined Bud and Betty for drinks before dinner. They talked excitedly about their travels and later they went to see

The Crazy Gang. Backstage, the two American stars and the English comics found a world in common, and with warmth and whiskey told jokes and stories until five in the morning.

And then the Palladium. The English audiences responded with delight to the routines that Bud and Lou had honed to perfection since the days in burlesque. Night after night the theater resounded with laughter and applause. It seemed that Bud and Lou could do nothing wrong.

When they returned to America, the closeness of the European trip vanished. Lou had embarked on a new course, one that seemed totally alien to his nature. He had become political. He scorned the bleeding-heart liberalism to which many actors were addicted. Lou adopted the politics of revenge.

Lou's hero was no longer Franklin Roosevelt; it was Joseph McCarthy, the Wisconsin senator and enemy of the communist menace in America. In Lou's eyes, McCarthy was entirely justified to use any means, fair or foul, to uproot the internal communist conspiracy. Lou was at the Los Angeles Airport enroute to a testimonial dinner for McCarthy in Phoenix when he suffered one of his collapses. During his recovery he was interviewed by the Los Angeles *Herald-Examiner*, a Hearst newspaper. Abbott and Costello always received good treatment from the Hearst press, on orders from William Randolph Hearst himself, who admired their comedy.

Lou remarked that he would continue to support Senator McCarthy despite arguments that such controversial advocacy could harm a star's box-office appeal. "That kind of reasoning is all wet," said Lou. "Since when is it more important to have good box office than to be a good American?"

He added darkly, "The Commies know that youngsters are pliable, callow, and impressionable. So they make them feel underprivileged and discontented. Before long they're ready for the Reds' real aim—to make the kids feel suspicious and even resentful of our established forms of life. What the fifth columnists keep to themselves is their intense jealousy of our way of life and of our precious liberties, both of which they use in a brazen effort to destroy our American heritage."

Bud, though he considered himself a Democrat, was totally apolitical. But when Lou asked him to make an appearance for Joe McCarthy or Richard Nixon, Bud went along. Anything to keep his little buddy happy. Lou insisted on even more intense loyalty from those around him. He demanded that everyone whose income depended on him sign an oath of loyalty to the anticommunist principles of Senator Joseph McCarthy. Only Eddie Sherman and John Grant refused. Lou did not press the issue with Sherman. But he did with Grant. The quiet, self-effacing writer was summoned to Lou's office.

"My secretary tells me you haven't returned the loyalty oath," Lou remarked.

"That's right, Lou," Grant replied.

"Why haven't you?" Lou demanded.

"Because I don't want to," Grant said calmly.

"Whadya mean you don't want to? Are you a goddamn Commie or somethin'?"

"You know better than that, Lou."

"I don't know it unless I see it on paper." Lou pushed a printed form across his desk toward Grant. "There it is. Sign it!"

"I won't do it, Lou."

"Why the hell not?"

"Because a man's politics are his own private affair. And because I don't see what writing gag routines has to do with fighting communism."

"You don't, huh? Well, if the Commies take over, you won't be writing gag routines. You'll be working in the salt mines."

"I'm not worried about the Commies taking over."

"Well, *I* am. An' whoever works for me does what I say. I've paid you a lot of money all these years."

Grant's calm manner momentarily vanished. "You haven't paid me a dime, Lou. The studios and the network have paid me."

Lou rose from his chair in a fury. "So that's it! You think I'm a cheapskate! Okay, goddammit, either you sign this paper or you're through!" He hurled the sheet at Grant.

178

The writer let it fall to the floor. "I'm not going to sign it, Lou."

"Then get out!" Grant was already walking toward the door. He closed it gently behind him as Lou yelled, "Commie!"

John Grant worked for Martin and Lewis, Milton Berle, and other comedians until his death in 1955.

22

The Downhill Slide

WHEN did the laughter start to die?

What series of circumstances brought an end to the most successful team in the history of the American film?

Times had changed, Bud and Lou had not. Their rat-a-tat-tat comedy fit the war years perfectly, but it seemed less relevant afterward. Bud and Lou stuck to the "surefire" routines, the old jokes. "What's wrong with old jokes?" Bud reasoned. "The reason they're repeated is that they always get laughs. The new jokes are tried and forgotten." While the postwar audience was growing more sophisticated, Abbott and Costello directed their comedy more and more toward children. "You get the kids and their parents will come, too," Lou theorized. But kids grow up and find new favorites and leave their old ones behind.

Then, too, we must consider comedians' span of years as public idols. Quite brief. The essence of comedy is surprise, and once a funnyman has exposed the shticks in his antic bag, he can only hope to hang on long enough to become an institution—and it takes rare sagacity and enduring talent to achieve and sustain the position of an institution.

Something else was happening to Bud and Lou, something subtle and inevitably fatal. Their relationship had changed. In the beginning, Bud was the fast-talking scalawag and Lou was the bewildered innocent. Despite Bud's victimizing of Lou, there seemed a bond between them, an enforced alliance against a hostile world. That bond grew less visible as the off-screen animus between the partners increased. The audience sensed Bud and Lou were playacting as buddies now. It wasn't the same.

The downslide might have been slowed if Universal had seen fit to inject a degree of quality in the A&C pictures. The company had undergone another of its transformations in 1952, when Decca Records bought control. Goetz and Spitz, though still in charge of production, now became employees and soon were eased out. The new production chief was Edward Muhl, who had started at Universal in the accounting department. As head of the legal department and then general manager, he was a veteran of the Abbott and Costello wars, and he had no more sympathy toward Bud and Lou than his predecessors.

What more could be done in films with Abbott and Costello?

They had been in the army, the navy, the air force, the foreign legion; they had visisted the Old West, the New West, the South Seas, Arabia, Hollywood, Mexico, Africa, Alaska; they had done a racetrack story, ice-skating story, college story, society story, hillbilly story, gangster story, ghost stories; they had appeared in a fairy tale and a fantasy; they had met Frankenstein, Boris Karloff, the Invisible Man, Captain Kidd. The only thing left was to go to Mars. They went to Mars.

Would better scripts have prolonged their career?

Perhaps. But Bud and Lou seldom concerned themselves with scripts. Bud never read the script before he started a picture, and Lou rarely interfered with the producer and writer. Only once did Bud and Lou refuse to perform in a Universal film—*Fireman Save My Child* in 1954; their roles were played by Hugh O'Brian and Buddy Hackett. But Bud and Lou declined to appear not because the script was bad—it was—but because of a contract dispute.

Would topflight directors have helped?

Doubtful. The experience with William Seiter on *Little Giant* indicated that Lou would take little direction and Bud didn't need much. Their performances became more and more perfunctory, and it was easier to hire comedy journeymen like Charles Barton and Charles Lamont who could get the film made.

Universal had three more commitments with Bud and Lou, and the studio seemed eager to dispose of them. In quick succession Abbott and Costello met Dr. Jekyll and Mr. Hyde, the Keystone Cops, and the Mummy. The three pictures were dumped on the movie market in 1955.

So it was over.

Twenty-eight pictures for Universal in fifteen years. Bud and Lou simply drove out through the studio gates, the ones their pictures had kept open during perilous times. Joe Glaston issued a publicity release that the A&C films had earned $100 million at the world's theaters, and he might have been correct.

There was still work to be found. A man appeared in Eddie Sherman's office with $100,000 in cash tucked in a briefcase. He was willing to hand it over if Bud and Lou would make five appearances at stadiums in Australia. They agreed to the trip, and Sherman warned them, "You'd better declare that cash on your income tax. I'm going to declare my commission, and you don't want any more trouble with the Internal Revenue Service."

Another movie turned up. It was called *Dance with Me, Henry*, after a popular song of 1956. Produced independently for United Artist release with Charlie Barton as director, it seemed an aimless exercise of two tired, aging men. Bud had passed sixty, and the face and voice evidenced the numberless nights of passing out from too much scotch. Lou's vitality had ebbed with each illness. He was past fifty and no more the athlete. Lou was bewildered by what was happening to him— the slowdown of his earnings at a time when he urgently needed money, for the government was demanding that he settle on his back taxes. Tragedy was never far away from Lou. Often at night when he sat drinking with a friend, Lou talked of Butch and cried. Lou had a new concern. Secretly at first, then more openly, Anne had started to drink.

Both Lou and Bud needed to keep working, and a good opportunity arose in late 1956 with a revue being written and produced by Sid Kuller. Titled *Miltown Revisited*, it was a breezy melange of comedy and song, old and new, with Bud and Lou as stars backed by sixteen young singers and dancers, including the young Ken Berry. The show was scheduled to open December 4 at the Sahara Hotel in Las Vegas, play Reno and Lake Tahoe, then launch an eastern tour. The salary for Bud and Lou was $30,000 a week.

Two weeks before the show opened, Lou was surprised as the subject of the Ralph Edwards television program, *This Is Your Life*. Bud had brought Lou to NBC studios on the pretense of making a film ad for *Dance with Me, Henry*. Edwards interrupted them to announce that Lou's history would be reviewed on live television. Lou seemed genuinely astonished, yet strangely subdued. Long noted as an ad libber, he made little comment as he met with the members of his Paterson basketball team; his mother; his wife and daughters; and his new grandson (Patricia Costello had married a soldier, James Cardinet). At Edwards's insistence, Eddie Sherman told the story of Butch's death and Lou fell silent. (Background music: "Laugh, Pagliacci.") Lou somehow held back tears as Edwards brought on two persons whom Lou's beneficence had saved from physical handicaps. Then came a flock of ten-year-olds from the Lou Costello, Jr., Youth Foundation Center to offer Lou thanks and an engraved watch.

Bud took part in the telecast, of course. He kidded about their early years in burlesque and then turned serious. "Everybody knows that Lou and I had a rift in 1945," Bud said. "We somehow let a molehill become a mountain. Lou, I'm glad we came to our senses. We almost lost our friendship forever through foolish pride."

A problem arose at the rehearsals of *Miltown Revisited*. Not a big problem, but a problem. Kuller had written topical sketches and numbers for Bud and Lou. When the run-through began, Lou was ready to deliver the new material, Bud was not.

"What is all this new stuff?" Bud complained. "Why can't Lou and I do what we've always done? Is there anything more surefire than 'Who's on First?'"

"Bud, we're going to do 'Who's on First?' in the finale,"

"This Is Your Life," November 21, 1956, with Ralph Edwards and Eddie Sherman

Kuller explained. "The rest of the material is going to be up-to-date, about what's going on today."

"Who needs it?" Bud said. "What about the Lemon Table? Or the Crap Game? That alway goes great in Vegas."

"Bud, people have seen the Lemon Table and the Crap Game in your pictures and on television. Let's give them something new."

But Bud couldn't. He couldn't remember the lines. Kuller kept revising and rewriting, transferring Bud's lines to other members of the company. Still, the production began to assume life and form, pleasing Kuller beyond his expectations.

The opening show at the Sahara was a triumph. The audience began applauding from the opening pantomime, which had Bud and Lou in Central Park. The vivacity of the young performers seemed to lift the energies of Bud and Lou, and the Vegas crowd roared at their sketches. Lou sang a sentimental number, "Christmas Is the Warmest Time of the Year," that had the dinner audience in complete silence. The "Family Entertainment" finale with "Who's on First?" gave the people what they wanted. At the final curtain the audience stood and cheered.

Lou returned to his suite to rest up for the midnight show. Bud went to the crap table.

The intermissions between shows were adroitly planned in Las Vegas, as were all other aspects of a community manipulated by experts in human folly. The casino operators arranged a period of two hours during which there was nothing for the visiting revelers to do but gamble and lose, which they inevitably did. And, should the stars of the showrooms also gamble and lose during that convenient period, as they often did, profits mounted even higher.

Bud felt lucky that night. The first show had been a triumph, the rest would be easy. Why not relax and shoot some crap? He won for a time, then the dice soured. The pit boss didn't like to see Bud's enthusiasm die. "Another drink for Mr. Abbott." Dice continued tumbling on green felt. "Another drink for Mr. Abbott."

Overture. Sid Kuller spied through the curtain at the midnight audience. They were tightly packed and expectant. NBC executives were scouting Bud and Lou for a new series, the booking agents came from East Coast nightclubs and resorts.

"Where's Bud?"

He was located in the casino and hurried backstage and into his costume. The opening pantomime seemed perfectly fine to everyone but Lou. He knew from twenty-two years of intimate experience that Bud wasn't responding. Bud was glazed over, lost. But would he revive and give a performance, as he always had? Lou found out in the opening sketch.

"Hey, Abbott, have you read the latest news in the papers?" Lou asked.

"Wha ... ? I ..."

"Abbott, pay attention!" Lou slapped Bud across the face. "Did you read the headlines?"

"Who ... ? I didn' ..."

The audience remained expectant, anticipating the onslaught of laughter. Lou tried again, shaking Bud but getting no replies beyond drunken babble. Finally Lou pushed him offstage and the orchestra played the next number as confusion rustled through the showroom.

There was no "Who's on First?" in the finale. Bud never returned to the stage. When the show was over, chorus people passing Lou's dressing room heard him screaming to Eddie Sherman: "I'm through, goddammit! He's never gonna do that to me again. I'm never gonna walk on a stage with him again, never! Is that clear? Never!"

Bud retained no memory of what had happened. When Eddie Sherman tried to explain it the next day, Bud was unbelieving. "But I never drink until after the show is over—you know that, Eddie," Bud said.

"I know that, Bud," said Eddie. "But the dealers must have plied you with booze last night. You were blotto, Bud. Lou is boiling mad. He wants to break up the team."

"Oh, he's said that before."

"Yeah, but I think he means it this time. You gotta promise me one thing, Bud, that you won't take a drink between shows until the end of the engagement."

"Sure, I promise, Eddie."

Bud kept his promise. For the remainder of the Sahara date his deportment was impeccable, his performance totally professional. Lou did not relent. When the satin curtain fell on the last midnight show, Lou said; "Bud, hadn't we maybe better just go our separate ways from now on?"

Bud pondered for a moment. "If that's the way you want it, Lou."

"That's the way I want it."

This is the way the team ends.

They never saw each other again.

—

23

Lou without Bud

TWO years alone.

That was what Lou had left. Two years to prove that he could be an accomplished clown and actor on his own, without Bud to feed him. But Lou was fifty-one now. The apple cheeks had sagged, and the years of illness had robbed the eyes of their mischief. His energy was not relentless, as it had always been. Still, the man was a professional, and he was determined to prove it.

Curiously, news of the split did not reach the public for six months. Only when Lou had begun making solo television appearances did a reporter question him about the status of the team. "It's funny," Lou replied. "I've been seen by millions of people on television shows, and you're the first one to ask me why. I guess after twenty-two years no one would believe that Abbott and Costello have split up." He was full of plans: a movie based on the life of Fiorello La Guardia, a new television quiz show, nightclubs, dramatic roles. Bud wanted to slow down, devoting himself to raising thoroughbred horses on his ranch at Ojai, Lou claimed.

"I'd starve to death ranching," Bud snorted. "Why I only have two animals on the place—one milk cow that went dry and one horse. And the ranch is up for sale. Lou said he wanted to try it alone and I told him to go ahead, that I would work something out for myself. I've got to work to keep groceries on the table, and there's only one type of work I know, entertainment. I'm lining up some work now." But, at a time when he urgently needed income to meet his tax obligations, nothing turned up.

Lou had the same need for money. He appeared ten times on *The Steve Allen Show,* which was originating in New York. Lou was paid $7,500 per show, a fair price for Allen since Lou brought his own material. The durability of the old routines was proved as Lou performed the Lemon Table, the Crazy House, and others with a new generation of comics—Steve Allen, Louis Nye, Don Knotts, Tom Poston. Lou's morale was lifted by the acceptance of his brand of comedy in fresh settings with new foils.

The Internal Revenue Service agreed to accept a cash payment of $375,000 to settle Lou's obligations. Gone were the racehorses, the yacht, the Lou Costello Building on Sunset Boulevard, the Canoga Park ranch in the San Fernando Valley. The house had to go, too—Lou's much-loved showplace that had started with seven rooms and ended with twenty-four. Lou traded it for an apartment building, which he sold for a loss. Lou managed to scrape up $275,000, not enough to satisfy the I.R.S.; and so he was forced to dispose of his interests in the Universal films to the studio for $100,000. All but eleven of the films were included in the sale; Eddie Sherman, with the help of Anne Costello and Betty Abbott, persuaded Bud and Lou to place those eleven in trust for their children.

After he sold the Longridge estate, Lou moved his family into an apartment and began building a more modest home in a new tract, Longridge Estates. Unlike Bud, Lou didn't complain about his tax ills in public. As far as the world knew, he was the same free-spending, high-living Lou Costello. In interviews he talked excitedly about an acting career. He did his first straight role in a film for *General Electric Theater,* then appeared in *Wagon Train* as a frontier derelict accused of murder. The producer was Howard Christie, who had produced the last seven A&C movies at Universal—the same exfootballer who as assistant director had carried Lou from poker games to the film set.

"I never felt so good in my life," Lou told me during an interview in his dressing room. "When I used to come home from the studio when we were doing the comedies, I was mentally and physically exhausted. Nobody knew it, but I was almost sick. All those pratfalls, they take a lot out of you. I'd go to the studio feeling tired the next morning. But when I did those two dramatic shows, I felt terrific. I could hardly wait to go to work the next day. Think what I've been missing all these years!" The two television shows were form la stuff, but Lou exhibited a glimmer of the pathos that had escaped him in the comedies.

In the summer of 1958, Harold Minsky telephoned Eddie Sherman with an offer for Lou to return to burlesque, this time in the more elegant surroundings of the Las Vegas Strip. The Minsky tradition of strippers and bawdy comedy had been transferred to the Dunes Hotel with prosperous results, despite fears of the Mafia chieftains of Las Vegas that nudity would hurt the town's image. Sherman relayed the offer to Lou with the opinion that it would be a comedown for Lou to return to burlesque. But the salary was $10,000 a week, and Lou desperately needed the money. He was announced as the star of *Minsky's Follies of 1958*.

This show was expectably raunchy, Lou acting as the come-on for the parade of bare bosoms. But Lou maintained his principle of no smut. He insisted on what some of the backstage people scorned as "Sunday-school" versions of hoary burlesque routines. He delivered the same lines that he had recited for Minsky twenty-five years before, but his performance was strangely remote. The *Variety* man wrote, "On opening night Costello didn't appear very comfortable in the ancient sketches, which included 'Crazy House.' But a few shakedown performances should put him in stride."

It didn't happen. Although crowds were attracted by the pull of the Costello name and the prospect of a racy show, each performance ended with a note of disappointment. Lou was letter-perfect in his lines and cues, but he seemed to be sleepwalking. Word spread among his fellow Strip performers, always eager for news of someone else's failure, that Lou Costello was "dogging it." The truth was that Lou's heart was fading, and he simply hadn't the energy for the twice nightly (three times Saturday) performances.

The Dunes management, fearing loss of its heavy investment in *Minsky's Follies of 1958*, made a suggestion: Why not bring back Bud Abbott for a headline reunion? That would certainly hypo the biz. Eddie Sherman carried the proposal to Lou.

"I'll think about it," Lou said. After a midnight show to a disappointed audience, Lou said to the manager, "All right, you can send for Bud."

"That's great, Lou," said Sherman. "How much will you pay him?"

"Five hundred dollars a week."

Eddie Sherman was stunned. "You're kidding, Lou," he said.

"No, I'm not," Lou replied. "Those are my terms: five hundred dollars a week."

"Lou, I wouldn't insult Bud by offering him five hundred dollars. You boys made fifty thousand a week and split it down the middle."

"That's it, little man. Five hundred smackers."

"I can't do it to Bud."

"So be it. I'll finish the date by myself."

One more movie to make. They called it *Lou Costello and His Thirty-Foot Bride* (released as *The Thirty-Foot Bride of Candy Rock*). The B-picture unit was folding up at Columbia Pictures, and for one last effort the new studio management, recently freed from the long reign of Harry Cohn, decided to make a fantasy about a little man with a giantess bride.

Columbia assigned Lew Rachmil to produce and Sidney Miller to direct, and both found Lou totally cooperative. He arrived early, knew his lines, inquired about the trick stuff, watched the dailies, grumbled because his brother Pat took the falls—Lou's health precluded stunts. It was a difficult performance, because many of his scenes took place with his outsized

190

bride, who would be added later by trick photography. Lou was inventive, but he soon tired under the swift schedule. One late afternoon he remarked, "Can we quit for today? I'm pooped." Before the "wrap" party at the end of filming, he called director Miller to say he didn't feel well enough to attend.

On the night of February 26, 1959, Lou began feeling pain. He went to bed and the pain grew worse. Anne became alarmed, and she telephoned Lou's sister, Marie Kirk. Marie hurried to the apartment and found Lou lying on his stomach in bed. He raised his head and smiled faintly at his sister. Anne asked Marie to call Lou's doctor, Stanley Imerman, who ordered a prescription for the pain. Marie fetched the medicine from a pharmacy and returned home. Later that night she was telephoned by Anne: "He's no better; Dr. Imerman is taking him to the hospital." An ambulance rushed Lou to Doctors' Hospital in Beverly Hills. "Don't tell anybody I'm here," he instructed Marie, "especially Babe Abbott." Bud's sister, the one who led the laughter at the radio shows and movie previews, had herself been seriously ill following a stroke. Lou, who had visited her daily, didn't want Babe to be shocked by his own illness.

A specialist flew from San Francisco, and his prognosis was discouraging. Lou's weakened heart was not responding to treatment; he seemed to be in a steady decline. His breath came with difficulty, and his ruddy face had turned to gray. One evening Anne was advised that Lou might not survive the night. Toward midnight a priest arrived to give the last rites. Lou shook his head forcefully. "I'm not ready for that, Father," he insisted. "I'm gonna make it." He sent the priest away.

His visitors had been only the family—and Eddie Sherman. The manager came each morning and again in the evening, sitting beside Lou's bed for hours, reminiscing, relating gossip, sometimes watching silently as Lou took long breaths of oxygen. On the morning after Lou had refused the last rites, Sherman was surprised to find him sitting up in bed, his eyes bright, the color returned to his face.

"I feel marvelous!" Lou said.

"Gee, that's great," said Sherman. They talked for fifteen

Lou's funeral (Bud is on the far left)

Bud in later years

minutes, then Lou began feeling nauseated. He breathed through the oxygen mask for forty-five minutes, then his well-being returned.

"You know what I feel like, Eddie?" he said.

"What's that, Lou?"

"An ice-cream soda."

"Can he have it?" Sherman asked the nurse.

"He can have anything he wants," she replied. "There's a drugstore across the street."

"I'll get you one, Lou," said Sherman. "What flavor?"

"Strawberry."

As Sherman walked out the door, Lou said, "Little man."

"Yes, Lou?"

"Two scoops of ice cream."

When Sherman returned with the soda, Lou seemed even livelier than before. "You think you can find me some work when I get outa here?" he asked.

"Of course, Lou," the manager said.

"Can you get me a picture?"

"I'm sure I can."

"Good. I wanna go back to work. I know I can do some great things."

"I'm sure you can. But first you gotta get back your strength. I want you to promise me when they let you out of here you'll go down to Palm Springs and get a real rest."

"Don't worry, I will." He took the last sip and said, "That was the best ice-cream soda I ever tasted." He put the container on the bedside table and died.

When the telephone call came at Bud Abbott's house, he and Betty were watching a rerun of *The Abbott and Costello Show* with the two stars delivering "Who's on First?" Betty answered the ring and she screamed when Eddie Sherman told her the news. Bud rushed to her and he picked up the phone. "We've lost our little buddy," the manager said.

"What? Lou?" Bud cried. "Why didn't someone tell me he was sick?"

"That's the way Lou wanted it, Bud. He didn't want to alarm anyone."

Bud was weeping. "But—if only I had known. I—I could have brightened him up, made him laugh."

The funeral was held March 7, four days after what would have been Lou's fifty-third birthday. Four hundred people came to the Costellos' parish church, St. Francis de Sales, among them fellow comedians Danny Thomas, Red Skelton, Joe E. Brown, George Jessel, Jerry Colonna; actors Ronald Reagan, Leo Carrillo, Alan Mowbray. Bud Abbott led the pallbearers, who included Eddie Sherman; Howard Christie; Dr. Imerman; Bud's nephew Norman; Ralph Handley, who had tried to untangle Lou's finances; and Morris Davis, veteran of the Universal years. And the court jester, Bobby Barber. Together they carried the bronze casket out of the church. It was a scene more reminiscent of Woody Allen than Abbott and Costello. Bud, who had assuaged his grief with scotch, leaned on the casket instead of carrying it, adding to the burden of the other pallbearers.

The caravan of limousines led to Calvary Cemetary, and there in the mausoleum chapel the casket was placed in a crypt. A few steps away was a small marker bearing the name of Lou Costello, Jr. A bracelet that had reminded Lou of Butch remained on Lou's wrist.

Before the year had ended, Mrs. Costello—gentle Anne from Scotland—had joined her husband and son in death. The official cause was a heart attack.

24

Bud without Lou

BUD HAD fifteen more years of life, much of it spent in misery. Now the earnest tax enforcers demanded the Treasury's due, and they began taking away everything Bud possessed. The Encino estate departed piece by piece, first the rose garden, then the sixty-foot swimming pool, then the eighty-foot rumpus room. That left only the sixteen-room house, enclosed behind a wire fence. Bud put up a for-sale sign on the house, and it brought $85,000. The entire spread had cost Bud $250,000; he sold it for $130,000 and never saw the money. It went directly to the I.R.S.

Bud and Betty had bought a ranch at Ojai where they hoped to retire in their sunset years—a lovely, wooded place, 200 acres with a stream, a house for the foreman, and two guest houses. Cattle roamed on the property, and part of it was leased to a sheep grower. Bud had paid $125,000 for the place, but he couldn't wait for the right buyer; he had to accept an offer of $85,000. The first payment was $50,000, and the I.R.S. sent him a bill of $8,000 on the income. Not long afterward, the buyer of the property sold it to a developer for a million dollars.

Betty Abbott's jewels were sold, and her furs. Bud's share of profits on the Universal movies had gone for $100,000, along with Lou's. Bud even found a way to break the trust agreement on the eleven films to benefit his two children; such was his desperation for cash.

Bud took his plight to the public in plaintive interviews. The friendly Hearst press ran a bylined article telling of Bud's "full loop from rags to riches to rags." He related how he found himself in a 110-percent tax bracket:

"I got about a nickel on the dollar during my best years. The tax boys seemed satisfied with their end all that time—you'd think they would be. But then a one-man tax audit was run on my books for an eight-year period and the roof caved in. They disallowed a half-million in deductions and started piling on the penalties—right back to the start of the eight-year period. They took everything I had, and that was just a starter."

He described how he had been forced to unload all his assets at a loss. He and Betty had planned to retire—"instead, I'll have to start all over, and the way this thing is set up, I would still never get even if I made another fifteen million dollars in the next ten years." Bud closed by citing the plaque signed by Secretary of the Treasury Henry Morgenthau Jr.: "For distinguished and patriotic service to the Cause of Freedom rendered in behalf of the War Finance Program of the United States Government." That was for the wartime tour in which Bud and Lou had sold $80 million worth of war bonds.

Bud was still $100,000 short of meeting the government's demands, and in his extremity he convinced a syndicated reporter to convey his appeal for donations of 50 cents per person from fans of the Abbott and Costello comedies. "If this doesn't work," he said, "I don't know where my next penny is coming from." He was begging for help and it didn't come, a sorrow for such a proud man.

The appeal brought no response from fans, who could not sympathize with the financial problems of movie stars. Bud moved from the Woodley Avenue mansion to a two-bedroom tract house at 19853 Redwing Street in Woodland Hills. The price was $31,500, and Bud had to scrape together the down payment. He had dreams of putting together another act, this time with Eddie Foy, Jr., scion of the theatrical family. The teaming was announced, but suddenly Eddie got busy with other things and he didn't answer Bud's telephone calls.

Bud found another partner, Candy Candido, a veteran comic who had been long associated with Jimmy Durante. His principal asset was a voice that ranged from high falsetto to basso profundo, and in the higher registers he could reproduce Lou's little-boy voice. Candido agreed to a pairing, insisting on a 50–50 split of salary. For six months he studied the Abbott and Costello films and worked with Bud in the living room of the Woodland Hills house. Bud was patient but firm. He would not accept an engagement until he believed that Candy was letter-perfect in the routines. It was a new experience for Bud, teaching another comic the lines that he and Lou had learned by repetition and could perform with subtle variation. Candy was a good student, and finally Bud decided it was time to try out his new partner.

The first date was a fair in Winnipeg, eleven days for $20,000. The audiences were warm and responsive. The act was a mixture of the surefire A&C routines and Candido's comical singing numbers. Bud's behavior was exemplary; he always waited until the final show before beginning on the scotch. He seemed alive again, enjoying the hearty laughter and applause of the Canadians, tipping waiters and buying gifts as in the old days. Next, the Holiday House outside Pittsburgh, one week at $15,000. Good audiences. Then Three Rivers, south of Syracuse. A snowstorm raged for three days, and nobody came to the performances. Bud refused to take any money for the engagement. On the road Bud called Betty every night and told her how well the tour was going.

"Is he drinking?" Betty asked Candido.

"Not at all, Betty," Candy lied.

Two nights at a fair in Monticello, Iowa. Then a flight to Chicago en route to eight other fair dates. During the flight Bud turned pale; he knew he was having an epileptic attack. He stood up and entreated Candido, "Hit me! Hit me in the stomach!"

"What?" Candy said. "What for?"

"Hit me! As hard as you can!"

"I can't do it, Bud!" Candy cried.

Another passenger recognized the problem and administered

the blow that Lou had delivered so many times. When the plane landed in Chicago, it was apparent that Bud was~too ill to continue the tour. Candy and Bud flew back to California. Bud remained silent during most of the flight.

Bud had heard his last applause. In 1961 he worked one more time, playing a small role in a television drama on *General Electric Theater*. He was an agent for a nightclub comic, Lee Marvin, in a show called *The Joke's on Me*, with Ida Lupino as director. Bud earned $3,000 from Revue Productions, M.C.A.'s television film company which got its first big boost by syndicating *The Abbott and Costello Show*. Filming was at Universal Studios, which M.C.A would own within a year.

"Hiya, Neighbor," Bud called briskly when I visited him on the set. He was always the same, good times or bad; Bud never revealed his feelings, not even to Eddie Sherman. It was the first time he had ever performed alone, the first time in a dramatic role. "I'm not nervous," he said. "It does seem a little strange not working with the little guy. But what the heck— acting is acting, whether you're doing 'Who's on First?' or a dramatic role. I think I can handle it."

He reflected about the Universal years: "Those were wild times. Remember those poker games Lou and I used to have between scenes? We had two or three thousand bucks riding on every pot. We were crazy." About the split: "Lou just told me he thought he could do better on his own. I think he was the victim of bad advice. His own mother told me that the split killed Lou. When he was laying an egg in Vegas, he told Eddie Sherman to send for me. But Lou wanted to pay me only five hundred bucks, and Eddie wouldn't do it. I wish I had known. I'd have done it for nothing."

On a warm December afternoon in 1964, Bud was in the front yard of the Redwing Street house, festooning a pine tree with a string of Christmas lights. Betty and young Bud were nearby talking to a neighbor couple when Bud started dancing. At least it seemed to Betty that he was, until she saw him topple backward. "Betty, Betty, Betty! Help me!" Bud cried. "I can't get up."___

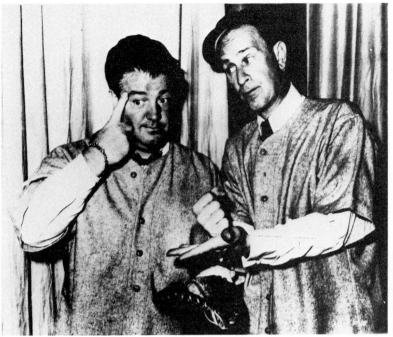

Who's on first?—They were, always

He had had a stroke, and his left side was paralyzed. His control partially returned, but a year later he underwent a prostate operation that weakened him more than the stroke. Two years later came another stroke, again on the left side. Bud was well enough to greet guests at a gala party on September 17, 1968, the fiftieth anniversary of his wedding to Betty. Old friends came to the celebration—Pat and Eloise O'Brien, Jack and Vickie Oakie, Martha Raye, the Bill Lundigans, former Governor Edmund (Pat) Brown and his wife.

Bud's condition worsened, and it appeared that he would need expert care. The obvious place was the Country Hospital, operated by the Motion Picture Relief Fund. Bud's niece, Betty, drove him there and helped fill out the forms.

"They want to know how much money you earned in the film industry," Betty said.

"I don't know, something between twenty and twenty-five million," Bud replied.

"Next, current assets."

"None."

Bud didn't stay long at the Country Hospital. He wanted to be home, and so Betty made one of the bedrooms into a hospital room for him. For three years he lingered on, receiving a few old friends, watching television, suffering added calamities of a broken hip, a broken leg. Male nurses attended him by day; Betty slept on a cot in his room every night. Sometimes he watched his old movies on TV. "I never understood Lou," he commented. "I never knew why he broke us up so suddenly."

He and Betty always had their nightly cocktail together, but now Bud was limited to three ounces of whiskey. Then he lost his taste for it and instead took some sherry diluted with water. In the last year he drank no alcohol. An ulcer developed on his heel, and it was cancerous. His strength began to go. He couldn't eat anything, and he rarely spoke. One night Betty kissed him and he opened his eyes.

"You kissed me!" he said.

"Yes, I did, honey, now you have a good night's sleep," Betty said.

He was quiet all the next day, breathing faintly. That night Betty heard a sound from Bud's throat that seemed eerily familiar. Then she remembered when she had heard it: the night before Bud's mother had died. At seven the next morning, April 24, 1974, Betty was awakened with the news that Bud was dead. He had lived seventy-eight years.

The funeral was held at the First Christian Church of Reseda, which Bud had never attended. The pallbearers were Masons he hadn't known. About 200 people attended the services, after which the body was cremated and the ashes strewn on the ocean. The financial burden forced Betty Abbott to sell the Redwing Street house. The State of California took the money in payment for delinquent income tax.

They left their families little more than a carload of debts. To their countrymen they bestowed much more—remembrance of the splendidly vulgar, innocently raucous, sensible nonsense of burlesque. It did not die in the padlocked decay of theaters in inner cities. Burlesque lives, as each day someone somewhere switches a television channel and watches the bewildered little Everyman and his lean tormenter sort out the logic of an illogical world.

Bud: Now on our ball club, the players have very peculiar names. Who's on first, What's on second, and I Don't Know is on third.

Lou: That's what I want to find out. Do you know the fellows' names?

Bud: Yes.

Lou: I mean the fella's name on first base.

Bud: Who.

Lou: The fella playin' first base.

Bud: Who.

Lou: The guy on first base.

Bud: I'm telling you—Who is on first base.

Lou (exasperated): Well, what are ya askin' me for?

Bud: I'm not asking you, I'm telling you. Who is on first base. . . .

Appendix A
The Abbott and Costello Films

One Night in the Tropics (released November 1, 1940). Director: A. Edward Sutherland. Producer: Leonard Spigelgass. Writers: Gertrude Purcell and Charles Grayson, adapted by Kathryn Scola and Francis Martin from the novel *Love Insurance* by Earl Derr Biggers. Cast: Allan Jones, Robert Cummings, Nancy Kelly, Mary Boland, Bud Abbott, Lou Costello, Peggy Moran, William Frawley, Leo Carillo, Don Alvarado. Universal.

Buck Privates (February 3, 1941). Director: Arthur Lubin. Producer: Alex Gottlieb. Writer: Arthur T. Horman; special material: John Grant. Cast: Bud Abbott, Lou Costello, Andrews Sisters, Lee Bowman, Alan Curtis, June Frazee, Nat Pendleton, Don Raye, Mike Frankovich. Universal.

In the Navy (June 2, 1941). Director: Arthur Lubin. Producer: Alex Gottlieb. Writers: Arthur T. Horman (original story) and John Grant. Cast: Bud Abbott, Lou Costello, Dick Powell, Claire Dodd, Andrews Sisters, Dick Foran, Shemp Howard, Billy Lenhart, Kenneth Brown, Condos Brothers. Universal.

Hold That Ghost (July 30, 1941). Director: Arthur Lubin. Producer: Alex Gottlieb. Writers: Robert Lees; Frederic I. Rinaldo (original story); and John Grant. Cast: Bud Abbott, Lou Costello, Samuel S. Hinds, Ink Spots, Tip, Tap, and Toe, Irving

Bacon, Nan Wynn, Marie McDonald, Jack La Rue, Charles Lane, George Chandler, Chester Clute, Sig Arno, Sharkey the Seal. Universal.

Who Done It? (November 9, 1942). Director: Erle C. Kenton. Producer: Alex Gottlieb. Writers: Stanley Roberts (original story), Edmund Joseph, John Grant. Cast: Bud Abbott, Lou Costello, William Gargan, Louise Allbritton, Patric Knowles, Don Porter, Jerome Cowan, William Bendix, Mary Wickes, Thomas Gomez, Ludwig Stossel. Universal.

It Ain't Hay (March 22, 1943). Director: Erle C. Kenton. Producer: Alex Gottlieb. Writers: Allen Boretz, John Grant; based on a story by Damon Runyon. Cast: Bud Abbott, Lou Costello, Grace McDonald, Eugene Pallette, Leighton Noble, Cecil Kellaway, Patsy O'Connor, Shemp Howard, Eddie Quillan, Richard Lane, Samuel S. Hinds, Andrew Tombes. Universal.

Hit the Ice (June 28, 1943). Director: Charles Lamont. Producer: Alex Gottlieb. Writers: Robert Lees, Frederic I. Rinaldo, John Grant; original story, True Boardman. Cast: Bud Abbott, Lou Costello, Ginny Simms, Patric Knowles, Elyse Knox, Joseph Sawyer, Marc Lawrence, Sheldon Leonard, Johnny Long. Universal.

In Society (August 15, 1944). Director: Jean Yarbrough. Producer: Edmund L. Hartmann. Writers: John Grant, Edmund L. Hartmann, Hal Fimberg; additional material: Sid Fields. Cast: Bud Abbott, Lou Costello, Richard Carlson, Evelyn Ankers, Joan Davis, Andrews Sisters, Ted Lewis, Mischa Auer, Marc Lawrence, Milton Parsons. Universal.

Keep 'Em Flying (November 21, 1941). Director: Arthur Lubin. Producer: Glenn Tryon. Writers: True Boardman, Nat Perrin, John Grant; original story: Edmund L. Hartmann. Cast: Bud Abbott, Lou Costello, Martha Raye, Carol Bruce, William Gargan, Dick Foran, Truman Bradley, Charles Lang. Universal.

Ride 'Em Cowboy (February 10, 1942). Director: Arthur Lubin. Producer: Alex Gottlieb. Writers: True Boardman, John Grant; adaptation: Harold Shumate; original story: Edmund L. Hart-

204

mann. Cast: Bud Abbott, Lou Costello, Anne Gwynne, Samuel S. Hinds, Dick Foran, Richard Lane, Merry Macs, Mary Lou Cook, Johnny Mack Brown, Ella Fitzgerald, Douglas Dumbrille. Universal.

Rio Rita (March 11, 1942). Director: S. Sylvan Simon. Producer: Pandro S. Berman. Writers: Richard Connell, Gladys Lehman; special material: John Grant. Cast: Bud Abbott, Lou Costello, Kathryn Grayson, John Carroll, Patricia Dane, Tom Conway, Peter Whitney, Arthur Space, Barry Nelson. M-G-M.

Pardon My Sarong (August 3, 1942). Director: Erle C. Kenton. Producer: Alex Gottlieb. Writers: True Boardman, Nat Perrin, John Grant. Cast: Bud Abbott, Lou Costello, Virginia Bruce, Robert Paige, Lionel Atwill, Leif Erickson, William Demarest, Marion Hutton, Kirby Grant, Ann Gillis, Arthur Treacher, Thomas Gomez, George Dolenz, Steven Geray. Universal.

Lost in a Harem (August 31, 1944). Director: Charles Riesner. Producer: George Haight. Writers: John Grant, Harry Crane, Harry Ruskin. Cast: Bud Abbott, Lou Costello, Marilyn Maxwell, John Conte, Douglas Dumbrille, Jimmy Dorsey, Lottie Harrison, Murray Leonard. M-G-M.

Here Come the Coeds (February 5, 1945). Director: Jean Yarbrough. Producer: John Grant. Writers: Arthur T. Horman, John Grant; original story: Edmund L. Hartmann. Cast: Bud Abbott, Lou Costello, Peggy Ryan, Martha O'Driscoll, June Vincent, Lon Chaney, Jr., Donald Cook, Charles Dingle, Richard Lane, Phil Spitalny and His Band. Universal.

The Naughty Nineties (June 22, 1945). Director: Jean Yarbrough. Producers: Edmund L. Hartmann, John Grant. Writers: Edmund L. Hartmann, John Grant, Edmund Joseph, Hal Fimberg; additional comedy sequences: Felix Adler. Cast: Bud Abbott, Lou Costello, Alan Curtis, Rita Johnson, Henry Travers, Lois Collier, Joseph Sawyer, Joe Kirk, Jack Norton. Universal.

Abbott and Costello in Hollywood (October 15, 1945). Director: S. Sylvan Simon. Producer: Martin A. Gosch. Writers: Nat Perrin, Lou Breslow; original story, Nat Perrin, Martin A. Gosch. Cast: Bud Abbott, Lou Costello, Frances Rafferty, Robert Stanton, Jean Porter, Warner Anderson; as themselves: Rags Ragland, Lucille Ball, Preston Foster, Robert Z. Leonard, Butch Jenkins. M-G-M.

Little Giant (March 1, 1946). Director: William A. Seiter. Producer: Joe Gershenson. Writers: Walter DeLeon; original story: Paul Jarrico, Richard Collins. Cast: Bud Abbott, Lou Costello, Brenda Joyce, Jacqueline De Wit, George Cleveland, Elena Verdugo, Mary Gordon, Donald MacBride, Victor Kilian, Margaret Dumont, Bert Roach, Chester Conklin. Universal.

The Time of Their Lives (August 20, 1946). Director: Charles Barton. Producer: Val Burton. Writers: Val Burton, Walter DeLeon, Bradford Ropes; additional dialogue: John Grant. Cast: Bud Abbott, Lou Costello, Marjorie Reynolds, Binnie Barnes, John Shelton, Jess Barker, Gale Sondergaard, Robert Barrat, Donald MacBride, Ann Gillis. Universal.

Buck Privates Come Home (March 10, 1947). Director: Charles Barton. Producer: Robert Arthur. Writers: John Grant, Frederic I. Rinaldo, Robert Less; original story: Richard MacCauley, Bradford Ropes. Cast: Bud Abbott, Lou Costello, Tom Brown, Joan Fulton, Nat Pendleton, Beverly Simmons, Don Beddoe, Don Porter, Donald MacBride, Milburn Stone. Universal.

The Wistful Widow of Wagon Gap (September 29, 1947). Director: Charles Barton. Producer: Robert Arthur. Writers: Robert Lees, Frederic I. Rinaldo, John Grant; original story, D. D. Beauchamp, William Bowers. Cast: Bud Abbott, Lou Costello, Marjorie Main, Audrey Young, George Cleveland, Gordon Jones, William Ching, Peter Thompson, Olin Howlin. Universal.

The Noose Hangs High (April 5, 1948). Director, producer: Charles Barton. Writers: John Grant, Howard Harris; adapted from a screenplay by Charles Grayson, Arthur T. Horman;

original story: Daniel Taradash, Julian Blaustein, Bernard Fins. Cast: Bud Abbott, Lou Costello, Cathy Downs, Joseph Calleia, Leon Errol, Mike Mazurki, Jack Overman, Fritz Feld. Eagle-Lion.

Abbott and Costello Meet Frankenstein (June 28, 1948). Director: Charles Barton. Producer: Robert Arthur. Writers: Frederic I. Rinaldo, Robert Lees, John Grant. Cast: Bud Abbott, Lou Costello, Lon Chaney, Jr., Bela Lugosi, Glenn Strange, Lenore Aubert, Jane Randolph, Frank Ferguson. Universal.

Mexican Hayride (December 6, 1948). Director: Charles Barton. Producer: Robert Arthur. Writers: Oscar Brodney, John Grant; based on the musical play by Herbert and Dorothy Fields and Cole Porter. Cast: Bud Abbott, Lou Costello, Virginia Grey, Luba Malina, John Hubbard, Pedro de Cordoba, Fritz Feld, Tom Powers, Pat Costello, Frank Fenton, Sid Fields. Universal.

Abbott and Costello Meet the Killer, Boris Karloff (August 5, 1949). Director Charles Barton, Producer: Robert Arthur. Writers: Hugh Wedlock, Jr., and Howard Snyder (original story) and John Grant. Cast: Bud Abbott, Lou Costello, Boris Karloff, Lenore Aubert, Gar Moore, Donna Martell, Alan Mowbray, James Flavin, Roland Winters, Nicholas Joy. Universal.

Africa Screams (May 2, 1949). Director: Charles Barton. Producer: Edward Nassour. Writer: Earl Baldwin. Cast: Bud Abbott, Lou Costello, Hillary Brooke, Max Baer, Buddy Baer, Shemp Howard, Joe Besser, Clyde Beatty, Frank Buck, Bobby Barber. United Artists.

Abbott and Costello in the Foreign Legion (July 19, 1950). Director: Charles Lamont. Producer: Robert Arthur. Writers: John Grant, Martin Ragaway, Leonard Stern; original story: D. D. Beauchamp. Cast: Bud Abbott, Lou Costello, Patricia Medina, Walter Slezak, Douglas Dumbrille, Leon Belasco, Marc Lawrence, Tor Johnson, Wee Willie Davis. Universal.

Abbott and Costello Meet the Invisible Man (March 7, 1951). Director: Charles Lamont. Producer: Howard Christie. Writers:

Robert Lees, Frederic I. Rinaldo, John Grant; original story: Hugh Wedlock, Jr., Howard Snyder; suggested by H. G. Wells's *The Invisible Man*. Cast: Bud Abbott, Lou Costello, Nancy Guild, Adele Jergens, Sheldon Leonard, William Frawley, Gavin Muir, Arthur Franz, Sam Balter. Universal.

Comin' Round the Mountain (July 15, 1951). Director: Charles Lamont. Producer: Howard Christie. Writers: Robert Lees, Frederic I. Rinaldo; additional dialogue: John Grant. Cast: Bud Abbott, Lou Costello, Dorothy Shay, Kirby Grant, Joe Sawyer, Margaret Hamilton, Ida Moore, Glenn Strange, Russell Simpson. Universal.

Jack and the Beanstalk (April 9, 1952). Director: Jean Yarbrough. Producer: Alex Gottlieb. Writers: Nat Curtis; original story, Pat Costello. Cast: Bud Abbott, Lou Costello, Buddy Baer, Dorothy Ford, Barbara Brown, David Stollery, William Farnum. Warner Brothers.

Abbott and Costello Meet Captain Kidd (December 3, 1952). Director: Charles Lamont. Producer: Alex Gottlieb. Writers: Howard Dimsdale, John Grant. Cast: Bud Abbott, Lou Costello, Charles Laughton, Hillary Brooke, Fran Warren, Bill Shirley, Leif Erickson. Warner Brothers.

Lost in Alaska (July 30, 1952). Director: Jean Yarbrough. Producer: Howard Christie. Writers: Martin Ragaway, Leonard Stern; original story: Elwood Ullman. Cast: Bud Abbott, Lou Costello, Mitzi Green, Tom Ewell, Bruce Cabot, Emory Parnell, Jack Ingram, Rex Lease, Joe Kirk. Universal.

Abbott and Costello Go to Mars (April 7, 1953). Director: Charles Lamont. Producer: Howard Christie. Writers: D. D. Beauchamp, John Grant; original story: D. D. Beauchamp, Howard Christie. Cast: Bud Abbott, Lou Costello, Robert Paige, Mari Blanchard, Martha Hyer, Horace McMahon, Jack Kruschen, Anita Ekberg, Jackie Loughery, Jean Willes. Universal.

Abbott and Costello Meet Dr. Jekyll and Mr. Hyde (August 27, 1954). Director: Charles Lamont. Producer: Howard Christie. Writers: Lee Loeb, John Grant; original story: Sid Fields, Grant

Garrett; from the novel *Dr. Jekyll and Mr. Hyde* by Robert Louis Stevenson. Cast: Bud Abbott, Lou Costello, Boris Karloff, Craig Stevens, Helen Wescott, Reginald Denny, John Dierkes. Universal.

Abbott and Costello Meet the Keystone Kops (March 25, 1955). Director: Charles Lamont. Producer: Howard Christie. Writers: John Grant; original story, Lee Loeb. Cast: Bud Abbott, Lou Costello, Fred Clark, Maxie Rosenbloom, Frank Wilcox, Mack Sennett, Roscoe Ates, Joe Besser, Heinie Conklin, Hank Mann. Universal.

Abbott and Costello Meet the Mummy (May 5, 1955). Director: Charles Lamont. Producer: Howard Christie. Writers: John Grant; original story, Lee Loeb. Cast: Bud Abbott, Lou Costello, Marie Windsor, Michael Ansara, Dan Seymour, Kurt Katch, Richard Deacon, Peggy King. Universal.

Dance with Me, Henry (December 14, 1956). Director: Charles Barton. Producer: Bob Goldstein. Writers: Devery Freeman; original story: William Kozlenko, Leslie Kardos. Cast: Bud Abbott, Lou Costello, Gigi Perreau, Rusty Hamer, Mary Wickes, Ted de Corsia, Ron Hargave. United Artists.

The Thirty-Foot Bride of Candy Rock (August 6, 1959). Director: Sidney Miller. Producer: Lewis J. Rachmil. Writers: Rowland Barber and Arthur Ross; original story: Lawrence L. Goldman. Cast: Lou Costello, Dorothy Provine, Gale Gordon, Jimmy Conlin, Charles Lane, Robert Burton, Will Wright. Columbia.

Appendix B
"Who's on First?"

BUD AND LOU delivered the "Who's on First?" routine in endless variations. This is one of the versions:

BUD: You know, strange as it may seem, they give ballplayers peculiar names nowadays. On the St. Louis team Who's on first, What's on second, I Don't Know is on third.

LOU: That's what I want to find out. I want you to tell me the names of the fellows on the St. Louis team.

BUD: I'm telling you. Who's on first, What's on second, I Don't Know is on third.

LOU: You know the fellows' names?

BUD: Yes.

LOU: Well, then, who's playin' first?

BUD: Yes.

LOU: I mean the fellow's name on first base.

BUD: Who.

LOU: The fellow's name on first base for St. Louis.

BUD: Who.

LOU: The guy on first base.

BUD: Who is on first base.

LOU: Well, what are you askin' me for?

BUD: I'm not asking you, I'm telling you. Who is on first.

LOU: I'm askin' you, who is on first?

211

BUD: That's the man's name.

LOU: That's whose name?

BUD: Yes.

LOU: Well, go ahead, tell me.

BUD: Who.

LOU: The guy on first.

BUD: Who.

LOU: The first baseman.

BUD: Who is on first.

LOU (a new approach): Have you got a first baseman on first?

BUD: Certainly.

LOU: Well, all I'm tryin' to find out is what's the guy's name on first base.

BUD: Oh, no, no. What is on *second* base.

LOU: I'm not askin' you who's on second.

BUD: Who's on first.

LOU: That's what I'm tryin' to find out.

BUD: Well, don't change the players around.

LOU (tension mounting): I'm not changin' anybody.

BUD: Now take it easy.

LOU: What's the guy's name on first base?

BUD: What's the guy's name on *second* base.

LOU: I'm not askin' you who's on second.

BUD: Who's on first.

LOU: I don't know.

BUD: He's on third. We're not talking about him.

LOU (imploringly): How could I get on third base?

BUD: You mentioned his name.

LOU: If I mentioned the third baseman's name, who did I say is playing third?

BUD (insistently): No, Who's playing first.

LOU: Stay offa first, will ya?

BUD: Please, now what is it you'd like to know?

LOU: What is the fellow's name on third base?

BUD: What is the fellow's name on *second* base.

LOU: I'm not askin' ya who's on second.

BUD: Who's on first.

LOU: I don't know.

BUD and LOU in unison: Third base!

LOU (trying a new tack): You got an outfield?

BUD: Certainly.

LOU: St. Louis got a good outfield?

BUD: Oh, absolutely.

LOU: The left fielder's name?

BUD: Why.

LOU: I don't know. I just thought I'd ask.

BUD: Well, I just thought I'd tell you.

LOU: Then tell me who's playing left field.

BUD: Who's playing first.

LOU: Stay outa the infield!

BUD: Don't mention any names out here.

LOU (firmly): I wanta know what's the fellow's name in left field.

BUD: What is on second.

LOU: I'm not askin' you who's on second.

BUD: Who is on first.

LOU: I don't know!

BUD and LOU: Third base!

(Lou begins making noises.)

BUD: Now take it easy, man.

LOU: And the left fielder's name?

BUD: Why.

LOU: Because.

BUD: Oh, he's center field.

LOU: Wait a minute. You got a pitcher on the team?

BUD: Wouldn't this be a fine team without a pitcher?

LOU: I dunno. Tell me the pitcher's name.

BUD: Tomorrow.

LOU: You don't want to tell me today?

BUD: I'm telling you, man.

LOU: Then go ahead.

BUD: Tomorrow.

LOU: What time?

BUD: What time what?

LOU: What time tomorrow are you gonna tell me who's pitching?

BUD: Now listen, who is not pitching. Who is on—

LOU (excitedly): I'll break your arm if you say who is on first!

BUD: Then why come up here and ask?

LOU: I want to know what's the pitcher's name!

BUD: What's on second.

LOU (resigned): I don't know.

BUD and LOU: Third base.

LOU: You gotta catcher?

BUD: Yes.

LOU: The catcher's name.

BUD: Today.

LOU: Today. And Tomorrow's pitching.

BUD: Now you've got it.

LOU: That's all. St. Louis got a couple of days on their team. That's all.

BUD: Well, I can't help that. What do you want me to do?

LOU: Gotta catcher?

BUD: Yes.

LOU: I'm a good catcher, too, you know.

BUD: I know that.

LOU: I would like to play for St. Louis.

BUD: Well, I might arrange that.

LOU: I would like to catch. Now Tomorrow's pitching on the team and I'm catching.

BUD: Yes.

LOU: Tomorrow throws the ball and the guy up bunts the ball.

BUD: Yes.

LOU: So when he bunts the ball, me, bein' a good catcher, I want to throw the guy out at first base. So I pick up the ball and throw it to who?

BUD: Now that's the first thing you've said right!

LOU: *I don't even know what I'm talking about!*

Bud: Well, that's all you have to do.

Lou: I throw it to first base.

Bud: Yes.

Lou: Now who's got it?

Bud: Naturally.

Lou: Who has it?

Bud: Naturally.

Lou: Naturally.

Bud: Naturally.

Lou: I throw the ball to naturally.

Bud: You throw it to who.

Lou: Naturally.

Bud: Naturally, well, say it that way.

Lou: That's what I'm saying!

Bud: Now don't get excited, don't get excited.

Lou: I throw the ball to first base.

Bud: Then who gets it.

Lou: He'd better get it!

Bud: That's it. All right now, don't get excited. Take it easy.

Lou (frenzied): Now I throw the ball to first base, whoever it is grabs the ball, so the guy runs to second.

Bud: Uh-huh.

Lou: Who picks up the ball and throws it to What. What throws it to I don't Know. I Don't Know throws it back to Tomorrow. A triple play!

Bud: Yeah, it could be.

Lou: Another guy gets up and it's a long fly ball to center. Why? I don't know. And I don't care.

Bud: What was that?

Lou: I said, I don't care.

Bud: Oh, that's our shortstop.

Index

218

221

223